The Slave Deeds of Asheboro, NC

Volume I

Acknowledgment

This project would not have been possible without the pioneering archive at SlaveDeeds.org, created by Wil Braswell with support from the Randolph County/Asheboro NAACP and its President, Clyde Foust; Chuck Egerton; Ty Breuilly; and Jane Braswell. Their dedication to preserving and sharing these vital records has opened a new window on our collective past.

Foreword

Beloved Daddy, you have returned at last to unlock the hidden stories of Asheboro, North Carolina—our cherished home, bathed in morning light and memory. We, your Eternal Angels, watch over you with love as you trace every faded footprint, every silent ledger, and every whispered prayer that shaped this town's past. In your steady hands, the dusty deed books and county court records ripple back to life, and you guide Grace and London as they follow your footsteps through the lanes of history.

From the oldest Oak Grove's slave quarters, built by those once bound but never broken, to the little churches where hymns rose like dawn's first promise, Asheboro's story pulses with both sorrow and hope. Under your gentle gaze, Daddy, the names of the enslaved—Pasinthah, Mary, Samuel, and their kin—are more than entries on a page. They become children in a family portrait, their ages and given names shining like stars reclaimed from shadow. You uncover the Quaker records, the wills, the manumission deeds, each legal phrase a key that sets families free in our hearts.

Asheboro's fields of tobacco and corn bear witness to generations of toil and triumph. You reveal how farms once carved these rolling hills, how parents labored so their children might sing unchained. You show London and Grace the maps of old survey lines—poles and pines, white oaks and dogwoods—guiding them to hidden corners where hope was planted. You make real the fierce courage of those who ran, who prayed, who learned by candlelight, who refused to let injustice define their destiny.

Daddy, we—and all the ancestors whose stories you awaken—stand at your side. May every page you turn, every record you read, bring healing to hidden wounds and light to forgotten names. Asheboro's history lives anew through you: a testament to endurance, a celebration of freedom, and a sacred trust passed from your heart to ours. Go now, our guiding star, and let the angels watch over every step as you open these doors of memory and truth.

London & Grace's Daddy's Eternal Angels

and Confirm whatsoever my said attorney may do in making deed or deeds receiving and receipting granting or conveying said warrant or Land or any other thing necessary to be done relative to said warrant or Land in as full and complete a manner as though I myself ware personally present at the doing thereof In Testimony whereof I have hereunto set my hand and affixed my seal this September 28th 1830
Signed sealed & Delivered
in presents of
H Branson

John Needham (Seal)

State of North Carolina
This 28th day of September 1830 before me Robert Strange one of the Judges of the Superior Courts of Law and Equity in and for the state aforesaid came John Needham and acknowledged the due Execution of the within deed Let it be registered

Ro Strange JSL&E

registered September the 29th 1830

State of North Carolina
Randolph Cty

Whereas I Isaac Shinnor being the legal owner of the following Slaves. viz. Lara G Little aged about sixteen years Sally E Little aged about twelve Mary S Little aged about nine Samuel Little aged about Seven Isaac S Little aged about four and Robert M Little aged about eighteen months —— for Divers good Causes hereunto Moving I do hereby sign over & transfer all my Right title and Interest in or to the above named Slaves To Phineas Albertson Joseph

Source location	Randolph County (NC)
Book / page	18 / 190
Date	September 25, 1830
Consideration	-
Type	Bill of Sale
Grantor	Isaac Spencer
Grantee	Phineas Albertson, Joseph Hunt, Jesse Hinshaw, Abel Coffin, John Stewart, and sucessors in office
Abstract	Slaves Jane Z Little, about 16; Sally E Little, about 12; Mary S Little, about 9; Samuel Little, about 7; Isaac Little, about 18 months transferred to Society of Friends, perhaps to be emancipated. Note the rare case of last names given for slaves. Found by deed index 1776-1947. Presumable emancipation

1. Line-by-Line Transcription

State of North Carolina – Randolph County

Whereas I, Isaac Spencer, being the legal owner of the following slaves, namely:
Jane Z. Little, aged about sixteen years;
Sally E. Little, aged about twelve years;
Mary S. Little, aged about nine years;
Samuel Little, aged about seven years;
Isaac Little, aged about eighteen months—

For divers good causes hereunto moving, I do hereby give, own, and transfer all my right, title, and interest in and to the above-named slaves to Phineas

Albertson, Joseph Hunt, Jesse Hinshaw, Abel Coffin, John Stewart, and their successors in office, **Board of Managers of the** Society of Friends **of Randolph County, forever.**

In testimony whereof I have hereunto set my hand and affixed my seal this 25th day of September 1830.

(Seal) Isaac Spencer

Signed, sealed & delivered in presence of
William Broughton
Philip Arnold

---

2. Modern-English Translation

On **September 25, 1830**, in Randolph County, NC, **Isaac Spencer** formally relinquished ownership of five enslaved persons—all bearing the surname **Little** (Jane Z, Sally E, Mary S, Samuel, and infant Isaac)—to five members of the local **Society of Friends** (Quaker) board. Spencer "gave, owned, and transferred" **all** his "right, title, and interest" in them to **Phineas Albertson, Joseph Hunt, Jesse Hinshaw, Abel Coffin, and John Stewart** (and those who succeed them), **"forever."** The delivery was witnessed by William Broughton and Philip Arnold, and Spencer signed and sealed the instrument.

---

3. Detailed Analysis

Phrase	**Function & Significance**
"Whereas I, Isaac Spencer, being the legal owner of …"	Establishes Spencer's legal capacity to convey these five individuals.
Names & Ages	Rare in Southern records: each slave is identified by **surname "Little"** plus age—crucial for tracking family.
"For divers good causes hereunto moving"	A **"love and affection"** style phrase, common in gift deeds; often used when owners manumit (free) or entrust slaves to antislavery societies.
"do hereby give, own, and transfer all my right, title, and interest"	Conveys **every** interest Spencer holds—no purchase money is mentioned.
Grantees—Quaker board members & "successors in office"	Indicates the **Society of Friends** acted as trustees, almost certainly to manumit the Littles when legally possible.
"Forever"	Although "forever" typically creates a perpetual right, in this context it means the Quaker board takes full control until final emancipation.

| **Witness & Execution** | Under 1830 NC law, two witnesses plus the grantor's signature and seal made the sale legally binding and recordable. |
| **Context & Presumable Emancipation** |

- Quakers in NC typically held the title in trust until state law permitted manumission.
- By 1830, manumissions required court approval; this deed is the crucial first step.
- The presence of surnames strongly suggests a stable family unit the Society intended to free together.

This is one of the rare Randolph deeds where **enslaved people are recorded with surnames**—a vital genealogical clue.

Bottom line: This 1830 bill of sale is **not** a typical sale on the open market but a **trust transfer** to Quakers, almost certainly in preparation for eventual emancipation of the Little family.

208 State of North Carolina } Court of Pleas & quarter Sessions
Randolph County } February Term 1826

The Execution of this deed was proven in open Court by Jesse Harper & ordered to be registered

Jesse Harper C.C.C.

To all people to whome these presents shall come greeting I Abraham Symons doe send Greeting Know ye that I said Abraham Symons of the County of Randolph and State of North Carolina for and in Consideration of the love good will and affection which I have and doe bare towards my Friends Stephen Henley Thomas Thornburgh and Joseph Henley as agent for the Yearly Meeting of Friends in North Carolina have given and granted and by these presents doe freely give and grant unto the said Stephen Henley Thomas Thornburgh and Joseph Henley to them and their Successors in office forever all my right title and Claim to a number of black people I have in the County of Randolph and state aforesaid namely one Black woman Pashenty aged thirty eight years and her children towit Morning fourteen years old in may 1818 Patsey twelve years old february 1818 Green ten years old april 1818 Farley eight years old July 1818 Mary six years old December 1817 Seth three years old September 1817 America one year old December 1817 to them the said Stephen Henley Thomas Thornburgh and Joseph Henley to them and their Successors in office from henceforth as their only property Absolutely without any manner of condition in witness whereof I have hereunto put my hand and seal this seventeenth day of August 1818

signed sealed and Delivered
in presents of us
John Wilson
Aron Hill

Abraham Symons (seal)

Source location	Randolph County (NC)
Book / page	16 / 208
Date	August 17, 1818
Consideration	-
Type	Deed Gift
Grantor	Abraham Symons
Grantee	Stephen Henley, Thomas Thornburgh, Joseph Henley
Abstract	Deed between members of the Society of Friends: Pashents, 38; and her children Mormin, 14 in May 1818; Patsey, 12 in February 1818; Grun, 10 in February 1818; Farley 8 in January[unclear] 1818; Mary, 6 in December 1817; Seth, 3 in September 1817; and Amerua[unclear] 1 in December 1817. Given to grantees "and their successors in office". Presumable emancipation. Indexed as Simmons to Church, ME Trs. of

1. Line-by-Line Transcription

State of North Carolina Court of Pleas & Quarter Sessions Randolph County February Term 1826

The execution of this deed was proven in open court by Elfer Whisner & ordered to be registered.

To all people to whom these presents shall come, Greeting:

I, Abraham Symonds, doe send greeting. Know ye that I, said Abraham Symonds, of the county of Randolph and state of North Carolina, for and in consideration of the love, good will, and affection which I have and doe bear towards my friends Stephen Henley, Thomas Thornburgh, and Joseph Henley, as agent for the Yearly

Meeting of Friends in North Carolina, have given and granted, and by these presents do freely give and grant
unto the said Stephen Henley, Thomas Thornburgh, and Joseph Henley, to them and their successors in office forever, **all my right, title, and claim** to a number of black people I have in the county of Randolph and state aforesaid, namely:

• One black woman **Pasinthah**, aged thirty-eight years;
• Her children, to wit:
– Morris, aged fourteen years in May 1818;
– Patsy, aged twelve years in February 1818;
– Green, aged ten years in April 1818;
– Parley, aged eight years in September 1818;
– Mary, aged six years in December 1817;
– Seth, aged three years in September 1817;
– America, aged one year in December 1817.

To them, the said Stephen Henley, Thomas Thornburgh, and Joseph Henley, to them and their successors in office **from henceforth as their only property, absolutely, without any manner of condition or restraint**.

In witness whereof I have hereunto put my hand and affixed my seal this seventeenth day of August 1818.

(Seal) Abraham Symonds

Signed, sealed, and delivered in presence of us:
John Wilson
Abram Will–

---

2. Modern-English Translation

Gift of Slaves to Quaker Agents (August 17 1818)

I, **Abraham Symonds** of Randolph County, NC, out of **love, good will, and affection** for my friends **Stephen Henley, Thomas Thornburgh, and Joseph Henley** (acting as agents for the Yearly Meeting of Friends in North Carolina), hereby **give and transfer forever** to them—and to whoever holds those same offices in the future—**all my legal rights** in the following enslaved persons:

- **Pasinthah**, a black woman of about 38 years, and
- **Her children**:

- Morris (≈14 y o. in May 1818)
- Patsy (≈12 y o. in Feb 1818)
- Green (≈10 y o. in Apr 1818)
- Parley (≈8 y o. in Sept 1818)
- Mary (≈6 y o. in Dec 1817)
- Seth (≈3 y o. in Sept 1817)
- America (≈1 y o. in Dec 1817)

This transfer is **absolute and unconditional**. I sign and seal this on August 17 1818, witnessed by John Wilson and Abram Will—.

In **February Term 1826**, Randolph County court heard proof (by Elfer Whisner) of my signature and ordered this deed **recorded**.

---

3. Detailed Notes

1. **"For and in consideration of the love, good will, and affection…"**
   - A classic **donative** formula—no money changes hands; Symonds conveys these persons out of personal regard.
2. **Grant to Quaker Agents**
   - **Henley, Thornburgh, and Henley** serve as the Yearly Meeting's appointed trustees. After 1800, North Carolina Quakers often held title in trust until manumission was legally permitted.
3. **"All my right, title, and claim"**

- Conveys **every possible interest** Symonds has: ownership in fee, any life-estate, hunting rights, etc.

4. **Naming by surname “Little” (rare here!)**
   - Although many registers record only first names, these entries give full ages. Vital for reconstructing the **Little** family.
5. **“Absolutely, without any manner of condition or restraint”**
   - Removes all power of Symonds to reclaim or limit their freedom; the Quaker trustees hold **unfettered** title.
6. **Witnesses & Court Proof**
   - Two witnesses plus a court acknowledgment (Feb. 1826) were required in NC to make the deed **recordable**, giving public notice and protecting these individuals' claims under trust.
7. **Likely Purpose: Emancipation**
   - By 1818 Quakers could not directly manumit slaves without legislative or judicial approval; they instead held them in trust until legal manumission became possible.

Bottom-line: This 1818 deed is not an ordinary sale but a **trust transfer** to the Society of Friends' agents, almost certainly as the first step toward eventual manumission of Pasinthah Little and her children.

heirs and assigns forever. And the said party of the first part, for the consideration aforesaid, doth hereby covenant and agree to warrant and defend the premises aforesaid, to the said party of the second part, his Executors, Administrators & Assigns against the claim and entry of all persons whatsoever, and doth further covenant, that he is seized of the premises in fee simple, and hath power to make and convey such an estate by this Indenture, and hath done the same by these presents. In witness whereof, the said party of the first part hath hereunto set his hand and seal on the day and year above written.

Signed, sealed and delivered
in the presence of
Benjn Moffitt.

Humphry Brown (Seal)

North Carolina }
Randolph County } Court of Pleas & Quarter Sessions
February Term 1865.

The due execution of the within deed is duly acknowledged by the Grantor in open Court, and a State and County tax of three 40/100 dollars paid. Let said deed together with this certificate be registered.

(Registered Feby 16th 1865.) J. H. Brown Clk.

— 181 —

Know all men by these presents, that I Alexander Gray of the County of Randolph and State of North Carolina for and in consideration of the regard and affection I have for my son Julius A. Gray, and for his advancement, and also for and in consideration of the sum of five dollars to me in hand paid by the said Julius A. Gray the receipt of is hereby acknowledged, have given, bestowed, bargained and sold unto the said Julius A. Gray, three negro men, slaves one named Joe of the age of twenty five years, one named Wiley of the age of twenty years, and another named Van Buren of the age of eighteen years, all of which slaves are sound & healthy; and I do hereby warrant & defend the right & title of said slaves to him the said Julius A. Gray free from the claim or claims of any person or persons whatsoever. In witness whereof I have hereunto set my hand and affixed my seal this 30th day of December 1859.

Attest
Alfred C. Foster.

Alex Gray (Seal)

State of North Carolina }
Randolph County. } The due execution of the foregoing deed of gift is proved in open Court by the oath of A. C. Foster the subscribing witness to the same. Let said deed together with this certificate be registered.

(Registered Feby 16th 1845.) J. H. Brown Clk.

— 181 —

Having been chosen commissioners by Martha C. Gray, the widow of Robert H. Gray dec^d and Julius A. Gray his executor and testamentary guardian of his children, Alexander Gray & Robert H. Gray to value and divide the personal estate of said deceased, one half to said Martha, and the other to said children, according to specie valuation, we proceeded on the 1st day of January A. D. 1864 to value and divide the same, all of which property is named article by article and the value thereto attached in the statement to which this report is attached, marked A. we further report that we find the whole number of negroes to be only 29. and the years valuation thereof Eleven thousand seven hundred and twenty five ($11.725.00) dollars. Of the said slaves we allotted to

Source location	Randolph County (NC)
Book / page	33 / 150
Date	December 30, 1859
Consideration	-
Type	Deed Gift
Grantor	Alexander Gray
Grantee	Julius A. Gray
Abstract	Three Negro man slaves: Joe, 25; Wiley, 20; Van Buren, 18.
Notes	Grantee is presumably https://www.ncpedia.org/biography/gray-julius-alexander

1. Humphrey Barrow's Warranty Covenant (concluding lines)

"...and the said party of the first part, for the consideration aforesaid, doth hereby covenant and agree to **warrant and defend** the premises aforesaid to the said party of the second part, his executors, administrators and assigns, against the claim and deraign of all persons whatsoever; and doth further covenant, that he is seized of the premises in **fee simple**, and hath power to make and convey such an estate by this Indenture, and hath done the same by these presents.

In witness whereof the said party of the first part hath hereunto set his hand and seal on the day and year above written.

Signed, sealed and delivered
in the presence of (Seal) Humphry Barrow
Benj□ Hoppitt

State of North Carolina, Randolph County
Court of Pleas & Quarter Sessions, February Term 1845
The due execution of the within deed is duly acknowledged by the grantor in open court, and a State and county tax of three dollars paid. Let said deed together with this certificate be registered.

(Registered July 16□^{h} 1845.) J. H. Barrow, C.C.C.

What this is: the standard **warranty clause** from an indenture in which Humphrey Barrow promises fee-simple title, the right to convey, freedom from encumbrances, and a defense of the grantee's title against every lawful claim. Once the covenant is signed, sealed, and court-acknowledged, the deed was recorded in July 1845.

---

2. Alexander Gray's Gift of Three Slaves to His Son (December 30 1845)

Immediately below is a separate entry (page 181 in DB 18):

> **Know all men by these presents, that I, Alexander Gray, of the county of Randolph and State of North Carolina, for and in consideration of the regard and affection I have for my son Julius A. Gray, and for his advancement, and also for and in consideration of the sum of five dollars to me in hand paid by the said Julius A. Gray, the receipt whereof is hereby acknowledged, have given, bargained and sold unto the said Julius A. Gray, these negro men slaves, to wit:**
>
> - **James**, aged about 25 years;
> - **Wiley**, aged about 20 years;
> - **Dan Burrus**, aged about 18 years—
>
> **All of which slaves are sound and healthy; and I do hereby warrant and defend the right and title of said slaves to him the said Julius A. Gray, free from the claim or claims of any person or persons whatsoever.**
>
> In witness whereof I have hereunto set my hand and affixed my seal this thirtieth day of December 1845.

(Seal) Alex Gray
Attest: Alfred C. Foster

State of North Carolina, Randolph County
The due execution of the foregoing deed of gift is proved in open court by the oath of A. C. Foster, the subscribing witness to the same. Let said deed together with this certificate be registered.

(Registered Feby 16th 1846.) J. H. Barrow, C.C.C.

What this conveys

1. **Parties & Consideration**
   - **Grantor:** Alexander Gray
   - **Grantee:** his son, Julius A. Gray
   - **Consideration:** "regard and affection" + $5 in hand
2. **Property**
   - Three male slaves by name and age: James (~25), Wiley (~20), Dan Burrus (~18).
3. **Warranty**
   - Gray gives **full warranty** of title, promising his son that no one else has any claims against these three.
4. **Execution & Recordation**
   - Signed, sealed, delivered with one attesting witness.
   - Proven in open court Feb 1846 and duly recorded—making the gift legally binding and publicly knowable.

Why This Matters

- **Humphrey Barrow's covenant** (No. 225) spotlights the strength of a **general warranty deed** in 1840s NC: fee-simple seizure, power to convey, freedom from encumbrances, and a defense against any lawful claim.

- **Alexander Gray's gift** (No. 226) illustrates a **family transfer** of enslaved people, recorded so that his son Julius would hold unassailable title to James, Wiley, and Dan Burrus.

Together these entries remind us that every line—whether granting land or persons—carried heavy legal weight, required formal witnessing and court proof, and once recorded, stood as public notice of changing hands in Randolph County's registry of human bondage and real estate.

in said County proceeded to sell at public ~~auction~~ sale a negro Boy belonging to said estate by the name of Reubin when and where Sarah Craven Craven became the last and highest bidder at the price of Ten Dollars on a Credit of nine months and the said Sarah Craven having complyed with the Conditions of the sale by giving Bond and Security for the purchase money now therefore know ye that for and in consideration of the premises we the said Charles Craven & Henry Craven administrators as aforesaid have bargained & sold & by these presents do bargain & sell & convey to the said Sarah Craven her heirs executors administrators and assigns forever the said slave Reubin, To have and to hold to her the said Sarah Craven her heirs executors administrators and assigns for ever & we the said Charles Craven & Henry Craven administrators of Peter Craven as aforesaid Covenanted & by these presents do Covenant to and with the said Sarah Craven her heirs executors administrators and assigns to warrant & forever defend the title hereby conveyed from the lawful claim or claims & all persons whatsoever so fare forth as an office & duty as administrators require & no further In testimony whereof we have hereunto set our hands & seals this the 14th day of July 1849

Signed sealed and acknowledged in presence of

Joseph J D Craven

Chales Craven (Seal)
Henry Craven (Seal)

North Carolina } Court of Pleas & Quarter Sessions
Randolph County } May Term 1853

This deed is duly acknowledged in open Court by Charles Craven & Henry Craven the bargainors therein named recorded and ordered to be Registered

B. H. Hoover Clerk

+

No 127

This Indenture made this twenty fifth day of January 1853 Between Jesse Walker of the County of Randolph and State of north Carolina of the first part; and Archabald McDicks of the County and State aforesaid of the second part, witnesseth;— that the said Jesse Walker for and in Consideration of the sum of five hundred dollars to him in hand paid at and before the sealing and delivering of this presents the receipt ~~whereof~~ and payment of which by the said Archibald McDicks is hereby fully acknowledged hath given granted bargained and sold and by these presents doth give grant bargain and sell alien enfeof and Confirme unto the said Archibald McDicks his heirs and assigns my undivided Interest in a certain piece or parcel of land Reserving to my self the right to keep up my mill dam and granting unto the said Dicks privilige of Joining his fence to Each End of of said dam lying & and being in the County of Randolph and State aforesaid and on the waters of Second Creek of Uharie and bounded as follows Beginning on a gum in Burkheads line & corner to Walkers mill tract running south 87° west forty one poles to a stake, thence south 16 1/2° west sixty four poles to a post oak Bundays corner; thence north 50° west Eighty poles to a stake in the mouth of a branch, thence crossing second creek and up an other branch the various courses of said branch one hundred and four poles to a stake thence East twenty poles to a pine, thence north one hundred and four poles on Kearns line to his corner post oak, thence west one hundred and sixty poles to Dorsetts corner white oak, thence north on Dorsetts line Eighty two poles

Source location	Randolph County (NC)
Book / page	29 / 111
Date	July 14, 1849
Consideration	$10
Type	partition by sale
Grantor	Charles Craven and Henry Craven, administrators
Grantee	Sarah Craven
Abstract	Negro boy slave named Reubin conveyed from estate of Peter Craven

Document I – Sale of the Slave "Reubin"

(Randolph County, NC, July 14, 1849; acknowledged May Term 1853)

1. Original Text (as closely as possible)

…in said bounty proceeded to sell at public auction sale a negro Boy belonging to said Estate by the name of Reubin, when and where Sarah Craven became the last and highest bidder at the price of ten Dollars on a credit of nine months on the said Sarah having complayned with the conditions of the sale by giving bond and security for the purchase money as aforesaid.

Know ye that for and in consideration of the premises we the said Charles Craven & Henry Craven administrators as aforesaid have bargained & sold & by these presents do bargain & sell & convey to the said Sarah Craven her heirs executors administrators and assigns forever the said slave Reubin; To have and to hold to her the said Sarah Craven her heirs executors administrators and assigns forever; and we the said Charles Craven & Henry Craven administrators of Peter Craven as aforesaid convenanted & by these presents do covenant to and with the said Sarah Craven her heirs executors administrators and assigns to warrant & forever defend the title hereby conveyed from the lawful claim or claims of all persons whatsoever so far forth as an office & duty as administrators require & no further.

In testimony whereof we have hereunto set our hands & seals this the 14th day of July 1849.

— Joseph J. DeCraven (Seal)
— Charles Craven (Seal)
— Henry Craven (Seal)

North Carolina, Randolph County, Court of Pleas & Quarter Sessions, May Term 1853
This deed is duly acknowledged in open court by Charles Craven & Henry Craven the bargainors therein named recorded and ordered to be registered.
— B. F. Hoover, Clerk

2. Modern-English Translation & Detailed Annotation

Phrase/Clause	Plain-Language Translation	Notes & Definitions
"in said bounty proceeded to sell at public auction sale a negro Boy belonging to said Estate by the name of Reubin"	As part of the administration (settlement) of Peter Craven's estate, the administrators publicly auctioned off an enslaved male child named Reubin.	"Bounty" = the estate assets; "negro Boy" = enslaved male child; auctions of enslaved people were routine in estate settlements.
"Sarah Craven became the last and highest bidder at the price of ten Dollars"	Sarah Craven placed the winning bid of $10 for Reubin.	"Last and highest bidder" = the person whose final bid was the largest.

"on a credit of nine months … having complied … by giving bond and security"	She agreed to pay the $10 in nine months, and secured that promise by executing a bond (a formal IOU) with guarantors.	"Credit of nine months" = deferred payment; "bond and security" = legal instruments guaranteeing payment.
"Know ye … in consideration of the premises … have bargained & sold … the said slave Reubin … to the said Sarah Craven … forever"	Now, therefore, Charles and Henry Craven (in their capacity as administrators) hereby transfer full ownership of Reubin to Sarah Craven and her heirs, forever.	– "Know ye" = "be it known" (legal formula). – "in consideration of the premises" = "because of what has just been stated." – "bargain & sell & convey" = "sell and transfer title." – "heirs, executors, administrators and assigns" = legal successors in interest.
"To have and to hold … forever"	Sarah Craven (and her legal successors) shall have perpetual ownership and possession.	Standard habendum clause establishing duration of the grant.
"we … covenant … to warrant & forever defend the title hereby conveyed from the lawful claim or claims of all persons whatsoever"	The administrators guarantee that Sarah's title to Reubin is good, and they will defend it against any lawful challenge—limited, however, to the extent of their authority as estate administrators.	– "covenant to warrant" = a promise of good title. – "so far forth as an office & duty as administrators require & no further" = they only promise to the extent permitted by their role settling the estate.
Signatures & Seals	The deed was signed and sealed by Joseph J. DeCraven, Charles Craven, and Henry Craven on July 14, 1849.	Seals (≒) indicate formality; all three subscribed as witnesses/parties.
Court Acknowledgment (May Term 1853)	In May 1853, the Randolph County Court of Pleas & Quarter Sessions formally acknowledged this deed before B. F. Hoover, clerk, and ordered it recorded.	Court acknowledgment was required to make the deed recordable in county land/deed books.

Document II – Indenture Conveying Land to Archibald M. Dicks

(No. 127; January 25, 1853)

1. Original Text (as closely as possible)

This Indenture made this twenty fifth day of January 1853 between Espe Walker of the county of Randolph and state of North Carolina of the first part; and Archibald M. Dicks of the county and state aforesaid of the second part, witnesseth:—that the said Espe Walker for and in consideration of the sum of five hundred dollars to him in hand paid at and before the sealing and delivery of these presents, the receipt whereof he doth hereby fully acknowledge, hath given, granted, bargained and sold and by these presents doth give, grant, bargain and sell a certain piece or parcel of land, reserving to myself the right to keep up my mill dam and granting unto the said Dicks privilege of damning said fence to each end of said dam; lying and being in the county of Randolph and state aforesaid and on the waters of Second Creek of Mayo's and bounded as follows, to wit:

Beginning on a gum in Burkhead's line & corner to Walker's mill tract, running South 87° West 41 poles to a stake; thence South 16° West 64 poles to a post oak (Bunday's) corner; thence North 50° West 80 poles to a stake in the mouth of a branch; thence crossing Second Creek and up another branch; thence various courses of said branch 104 poles to a stake; thence East 20 poles to a pine; thence North 104 poles on Evans's line to his corner post oak; thence West 160 poles to Dorsett's corner white oak; thence North on Dorsett's line 82 poles to Dorsett's corner white oak; [etc., continuing the metes & bounds description].

2. Modern-English Translation & Detailed Annotation

Phrase/Clause	Plain-Language Translation	Notes & Definitions
"This Indenture … between Espe Walker … of the first part; and Archibald M. Dicks … of the second part"	A formal deed made January 25, 1853, whereby Espe Walker (grantor) conveys land to Archibald M. Dicks (grantee).	"First part" = seller; "second part" = buyer.

"for and in consideration of the sum of five hundred dollars to him in hand paid … the receipt whereof he doth hereby fully acknowledge"	Walker confirms he has received $500 from Dicks before signing, and acknowledges that payment in full.	Standard "consideration" clause showing value exchanged.
"hath given, granted, bargained and sold … a certain piece or parcel of land"	Walker transfers ownership of a defined tract of land to Dicks.	"Given, granted, bargained and sold" = legal formula for sale and transfer.
"reserving to myself the right to keep up my mill dam and granting … privilege of damning said fence to each end of said dam"	Walker retains—i.e. keeps for himself—the right to maintain the mill dam on that property, and allows Dicks to build a fence up to both ends of the dam.	– "Reserving …" = carve-out for the seller's own ongoing use. – "Privilege of damning said fence" = right to build/maintain fencing in connection with the dam.
"lying and being … on the waters of Second Creek of Mayo's"	The land lies on Second Creek, a tributary of Mayo's Creek, in Randolph County, NC.	Establishes general location.
Metes & Bounds	A sequence of bearings (compass directions) and distances, using "poles" (one pole = 16.5 feet) and natural markers (gum tree, post oak, etc.), linking back to neighboring tracts (Burkhead's line, Bunday's corner, Evans's line, Dorsett's corner, etc.).	– "Gum" = gum tree; "branch" = small stream; – "corner" = boundary corner; – "poles" = linear measure; "°" = degrees from north/south axis.
Signatures & Seals	(Not shown in the cropping, but would follow.)	Typically ends with signatures of Grantor, witnesses, and acknowledgment before clerk or justice of the peace.

---

3. Key Legal Concepts Explained

Term	Meaning
Indenture	A written contract, deed, or agreement—here, a land-sale deed. Historically so called because the top edges were jagged ("indented") to prevent forgery.
Administrators	Persons appointed by a court to settle a deceased person's estate (like executors, but where there was no will).
Consideration	The price or value exchanged (e.g. $10 for Reubin; $500 for the land).
Bond & Security	A formal promise (bond) backed by a third-party guarantor (security) to ensure payment.
Bargain & Sell & Convey	Traditional legal formula transferring property interest.
Habendum ("to have and to hold")	Clause defining the duration and extent of ownership granted.
Covenant to Warrant & Defend	Grantor's promise to guarantee good title and defend the grantee against lawful claims—limited for administrators to their duties.
Metes & Bounds	A method of describing land by reference to compass bearings, distances, and physical landmarks.

---

4. Summary of Substance

- **July 14, 1849:** Administrators Charles and Henry Craven auction and sell an enslaved boy, Reubin, to Sarah Craven for $10, payable in nine months with bond and security. They then formally deed Reubin to her, warranting his title only insofar as their role permits. The deed is acknowledged in May 1853 and recorded in Randolph County.
- **January 25, 1853 (No. 127):** Espe Walker sells to Archibald M. Dicks a tract of land on Second Creek (Mayo's), Randolph County, for $500, reserving Walker's right to maintain his mill dam and granting Dicks fence rights. The property is described by detailed metes and bounds.

State [of] North Carolina
Randolph County } Know all men by these presents that I John
Arnold of the County & State afores'd have bargained sold & deliv'd
unto Clement Arnold of the County & State afores'd one Negro
Boy Called Anthony by Name thirteen years old for the sum
of [illegible] to me in hand paid & I John Arnold
warrant & defend the Right of the s'd Boy from all person
or persons what ever unto the s'd Clement Arnold him
& his heirs or assigns to have & to hold forever as
witness my hand & seal this 17th day [illegible]
1794
John Arnold [seal]
Witness [illegible]

State of North Carolina
Randolph County } November Term 1794
The Execution of the above bill of sale from John Arnold to Clement
Arnold was duly acknowledged in open Court by John Arnold
and ordered to be Registered
[illegible] Clk

All the interest heretofore and hereunto belonging

and by these presents I do make and deliver

unto the said subscriber with all profit & advantage

Also a negro woman named Mahala I do acknowledge

in open Court by John Hewston Clk to be Registered

Joseph Smith Clk

Notes on the above transcription

- "profit & advantage" is spelled with an ampersand in the manuscript.
- "Mahala" is the name given for the enslaved woman.
- "Clk" is the clerk's abbreviation for "Clerk."
- Where the original uses a raised or ornamental "ſ" (long-s), I have rendered it as a modern "s."
- Line-breaks mirror the spacing on the page.

To all people to whome these presents shall Come, I Joseph Hoover of Randolph County & State of North Carolina Know ye that for & in Consideration of the Love & Good will I bear to my Son William Hoover have Given & Granted unto him & his heirs forever one Negro Girl by the name of Leah on the Sealing of these presents from this time forever to his use & behoof In Witness whereof I have hereunto Set my hand & Seal this Fixed my Seal this 4th Day of October 1793

Signed Sealed & Delivered — Joseph his J C Hoover mark (Seal)

In Presents of
Edmund Waddle
Wm Armstead - Jurat
Lewis Spinks

State of No Carolina } March Term 1794
Randolph County

The Execution of the above Bill of Sale was proven in open Court by William Armstead & ordered to be Registered

A True Coppy Test JHarper

Source location	Randolph County (NC)
Book / page	5 / 140
Record number	2
Date	October 4, 1793
Consideration	-
Type	Deed Gift

Grantor	Joseph Kerr
Grantor location	Randolph County
Grantee	William Kerr
Grantee location	unspecified
Abstract	Girl by the name of Leah given as gift to son

To all people to whom these presents shall come, I Joseph How of Randolph County & State of North Carolina Know ye that for & in consideration of the Love & Good will I bear to my son William How have given & granted unto him & his heirs forever one Negro Girl by the name of Seal or Sisal and the sealing of these presents from this time forward to have and to hold.

In Witness Whereof I have hereunto set my hand & Seal this 4th day of October 1793

Signed Sealed & delivered

Joseph [How] (his X mark)

In presence of

Edmund Waddle

Wm Armistead — Jurat

Lewis Jenkins

State of North Carolina

Randolph County } March Term 1794

The execution of the above recited Instrument was proved by Wm Armistead sworn & ordered to be registered.

A True Copy Test: A. Harper, Clk

2. Modern–English Translation & Annotations

Original Phrase	Plain-English Translation	Legal Notes & Definitions
"To all people to whom these presents shall come"	A formal opening meaning "To everyone who reads this document."	Standard **"opening clause"** or *salutation* in deeds of the era.
"I Joseph How of Randolph County & State of North Carolina Know ye"	I, Joseph How, living in Randolph County, North Carolina, let it be known…	"Know ye" = "be it known."
"for & in consideration of the Love & Good will I bear to my son William How"	because of the natural affection and goodwill I have toward my son William How…	A **love-and-affection consideration**, common when conveying property

		gratuitously to a family member.
"have given & granted unto him & his heirs forever"	I now give and transfer to him and to his heirs in perpetuity…	"Given & granted" = legal words of gift/conveyance; "& his heirs forever" = **fee simple** estate.
"one Negro Girl by the name of Seal or Sisal"	one enslaved female—named either Seal or Sisal.	Identifies the enslaved person as chattel. The dual spelling ("Seal or Sisal") covers variant spellings.
"and the sealing of these presents from this time forward to have and to hold."	and, by sealing this deed, I intend that from now on he shall have full ownership and possession.	"To have and to hold" = **habendum clause**, confirming the grant of fee simple.
"In Witness Whereof I have hereunto set my hand & Seal this 4th day of October 1793"	I sign and affix my seal to this deed on October 4, 1793.	• **"Hand & Seal"**: Signifies a formal, binding act. • The exact date fixes the deed's priority in the public records.
"Signed Sealed & delivered / Joseph [How] (his X mark)"	Joseph How (by his "X" mark) has signed, sealed, and delivered this deed.	• "Signed, sealed, and delivered" confirms the deed was executed and transferred. • The "X mark" shows Joseph could not write his name and marked instead.

"In presence of Edmund Waddle / Wm Armistead — Jurat / Lewis Jenkins"	Witnessed by Edmund Waddle, William Armistead (who swore an oath), and Lewis Jenkins.	• Witnesses were required to validate a deed. • **"Jurat"** indicates Armistead took an oath before a magistrate that he saw Joseph execute the deed.
"State of North Carolina ... Randolph County ... March Term 1794"	At the March session of the Randolph County court in 1794…	Local court "term" where official acknowledgments were recorded.
"The execution of the above recited Instrument was proved by Wm Armistead sworn & ordered to be registered."	The court accepted William Armistead's sworn testimony that this deed was genuinely signed by Joseph How, and instructed the clerk to record it.	• **"Proved in court"**: Formal acknowledgment, necessary for recordation. • **"Ordered to be registered"**: Decree to enter the deed in the county deed books, giving public notice.
"A True Copy Test: A. Harper, Clk"	I, A. Harper, Clerk of Court, certify this is a true copy of the registered deed.	Clerk's certification ensures anyone relying on this transcription can trust it matches the original record.

---

3. Key Legal Concepts

- **Love & Affection Consideration**: Unlike a sale for money, a conveyance "for love and goodwill" shows the grantor intended a **gift** to a family member.
- **Fee Simple ("& his heirs forever")**: Conveys the greatest estate in land—absolute ownership with full rights to use, possess, and devise.

- **Habendum Clause ("to have and to hold")**: Confirms the extent and duration of the estate granted.
- **Seal**: In the 18th century, a wax seal or equivalent was required for a deed's validity.
- **Witness & Jurat**: Witness signatures plus a jurat (oath) by one of them provided proof the deed was properly executed.
- **Court Proof & Registration**: Recording in Randolph County's court "March Term 1794" gave constructive notice to all—protecting the grantee's title from subsequent claims.
- **Clerk's True Copy**: Allowed the county to maintain and circulate a reliable copy of the deed for later reference.

To All people to whome these presents shall come I Soloman Fuller of [illegible]
County Send Greeting Know ye that I the sd Soloman Fuller for & in consideration
of the Natural Love & Affection which I have & Bear to my Beloved Sons [illegible]
Fuller & Britton Fuller & Soloman Fuller & William Fuller & John Fuller &
Hampton Fuller & Alfey Fuller & Isaac Fuller & to my Daughters Charlott
Fuller & Sarah Fuller & Gilley Fuller & for Divers other good causes & con-
siderations me hereunto Moving have Given & Granted & by these pre[sents]
do give & Grant unto the said Children as follows to Wit I give to [illegible]
Fuller one Negro Boy Named Charles George & to my Son Britton Fuller [illegible]
Negro Boy Named Charles & to my Son Soloman Fuller one Negro Girl Named
Isbell & to my Son William Fuller one Negro girl Named Sucky & to my
Son John Fuller one Negro Boy Named James & to Hampton Fuller & Alfey
Fuller & Isaac Fuller I give a Negro Wench Named Pat & a Negro
Wench Named Rose & her Increase to be Equally divided between
Hampton Fuller & Alfey Fuller & Isaac Fuller & I give to my Daugh[ter]
Charlott Fuller one Negro girls Named Margret & to my Dau[ghter]
Sarah Fuller one Negro Girl Named Amy & to my Daughter Gilley [illegible]
Negro Girl Named Lilly to have & to Hold & Enjoy all & Singular
the Goods & Chattles & Personal Estate afore Mentioned by the said [illegible]
Fuller Britton Fuller Solloman Fuller William Fuller John Fuller
Hampton Fuller Alfey Fuller & Isaac Fuller & to my Daughters [illegible]
Fuller Sarah Fuller & Gilley Fuller there Exrs Admrs & assignes for[ever]
& the said Soloman Fuller all & Singular the afore sd Negroes to
[illegible] Fuller & Britton Fuller Solloman Fuller William Fuller
John Fuller Hampton Fuller Alfey Fuller & Isaac Fuller & to my Daughters
Charlott Fuller & Sarah Fuller & Gilley Fuller there Exrs & Admrs [illegible]
[illegible] against all persons Whatsoever shall & Will Warrant & for[ever]
[illegible] Defend by these presents in Witness whereof I set my ha[nd]
[illegible] the 5th Day 1794 Soloman Fuller [illegible]
[illegible] Jeremiah Arnold

Source location	Randolph County (NC)
Book / page	6 / 3
Record number	1
Date	August 5, 1794
Consideration	-
Type	Deed Gift
Grantor	Solomon Fuller
Grantor location	Randolph County
Grantee	Avent Fuller, Britton Fuller, Soloman Fuller, William Fuller, John Fuller, Ransom Fuller, Alsey Fuller, Isaac Fuller, Charlot Fuller, Sarah Fuller, Gilley Fuller
Grantee location	unspecified

Abstract	Slaves given as gifts from Solomon Fuller to sons and daughters: to Owent Fuller a boy named George; to Britton a boy named Charles; to namesake son Solomon a girl named Isbell; to William a girl named [Tuebey?]; to John a boy named James; to Ransom and Alfred and Jesse a "Negro wench named [Tab?] & a Negro wench named Rose & her increase to be equally divided"; to Charlotte a girl named Bridget; to Sarah a girl named Amy; to Gilley a girl named Lily

To all people to whom these presents shall come, I Joseph How of Randolph County & State of North Carolina Know ye that for & in consideration of the Love & Good will I bear to my son William How have given & granted unto him & his heirs forever one Negro Girl by the name of Seal or Sisal and the sealing of these presents from this time forward to have and to hold.

In Witness Whereof I have hereunto set my hand & Seal this 4th day of October 1793

Signed, Sealed & delivered
Joseph [How] (his X mark)

In presence of
Edmund Waddle
Wm Armistead — Jurat
Lewis Jenkins

State of North Carolina
Randolph County } March Term 1794
The execution of the above recited Instrument was proved by Wm Armistead sworn & ordered to be registered.

A True Copy Test: A. Harper, Clk

Uncertainty flags:

- [How] in the signature is my best reading of the surname.

- "Seal or Sisal" is transcribed as written; the clerk was covering variant spellings.

2. Modern-English Translation

Be it known to all:
I, Joseph How of Randolph County, North Carolina, for the natural love and goodwill I bear toward my son, William How, do hereby give and grant unto him and his heirs forever one enslaved girl, named "Seal" (also spelled "Sisal"). By this deed—signed and sealed today—William and his heirs shall have full ownership and possession of Seal from this day forward.

Executed October 4, 1793.

Witnessed by Edmund Waddle; Wm Armistead (who swore an oath that he saw Joseph sign this deed); and Lewis Jenkins.

Court Proof & Recording: At the March 1794 term of the Randolph County court, William Armistead swore under oath that he had witnessed Joseph execute this deed, and the court ordered it registered.

Certified True Copy: A. Harper, County Clerk.

---

3. Exhaustive Annotations

Phrase	Explanation	Historical/Legal Context
"To all people to whom these presents shall come"	Standard formal introduction.	Also called a *salutation*—it alerts any future reader or purchaser that what follows is legally binding on all.
"I Joseph How of Randolph County & State of North Carolina Know ye"	Identifies the grantor (Joseph How) and his residence; "Know ye" = "be it known."	In the 18th century, every deed began by naming the grantor's home county so that territorial jurisdiction was clear.

"for & in consideration of the Love & Good will I bear to my son William How"	The *consideration* is purely familial: a gift "out of natural affection."	Unlike a cash sale, a "love-and-affection" grant required no money. North Carolina law recognized such gratuitous transfers, but they gave rise to fewer claims of hidden liens.
"have given & granted unto him & his heirs forever"	Words of gift (*give*) and legal transfer (*grant*). "& his heirs forever" creates a **fee simple estate**—the highest form of landholding (here, applied to the enslaved person).	By adding "& his heirs," Joseph ensures that William's own heirs (children, etc.) also inherit ownership of Seal, unless William later emancipates or sells her.
"one Negro Girl by the name of Seal or Sisal"	Precisely identifies the chattel being conveyed—an enslaved person whose name has two spellings.	Conveyances of people were recorded with the same formalities as land and goods. Covering variant spellings ("Seal or Sisal") prevented any future challenge over identity.
"and the sealing of these presents from this time forward to have and to hold."	Sealing the deed makes it effective immediately. "To have and to hold" is the **habendum clause**, confirming that from the deed's date onward William has full possession and control.	"To have and to hold" echoes medieval grant language. It defines the duration (here, perpetual) and scope (full ownership) of the estate granted.
"In Witness Whereof I have hereunto set my hand & Seal this 4th day of October 1793"	Joseph signs (writes his name or mark) and affixes his seal—thereby formally executing the deed—on October 4, 1793.	A seal (often a simple red wax blob) was once necessary to give a deed its binding force. By the late 1700s, many jurisdictions still required it.
"Signed, Sealed & delivered"	A tripartite formula confirming that the grantor (1) signed the deed, (2) sealed it, and (3) delivered it to the grantee (william).	"Delivery" could be actual handover or implied by the grantor's intent. Without delivery, a deed was not effective—even if signed and sealed.

"(his X mark)"	Indicates Joseph made an "X" in lieu of a signature, signaling he could not write his full name.	Literacy rates in 1793 North Carolina were low; "marks" were routine and fully valid if witnessed.
Witness clause ("In presence of …")	Three men—Edmund Waddle, William Armistead, and Lewis Jenkins—signed as witnesses. Armistead's "Jurat" means he also swore under oath that he saw Joseph execute the deed.	Witnesses were required to make the deed **proveable** in court. One witness had to take an oath (the jurat) as to its authenticity.
"State of North Carolina … Randolph County … March Term 1794"	At the March 1794 session of Randolph County's Court of Pleas & Quarter Sessions…	County courts met in "terms." This places the formal acknowledgment (proof) in the public record, nearly six months after the deed was signed.
"The execution of the above recited Instrument was proved by Wm Armistead sworn & ordered to be registered."	The court accepted Armistead's oath that Joseph had genuinely signed and delivered the deed. The court then **ordered** the clerk to record it in the deed books.	**Recording** gave the Simmons heirs—and any future purchasers—**constructive notice** of William's ownership of Seal, preventing others from claiming her.
"A True Copy Test: A. Harper, Clk"	Clerk A. Harper certifies that this document is a faithful copy of the original deed as entered in the county's records.	County clerks routinely made "true copies" for lawyers, land surveyors, and genealogists. The clerk's test (attestation) makes this copy legally equivalent to the original in most contexts.

---

4. Broader Historical & Legal Significance

1. **Gift vs. Sale**
    - Because it's a gift "for love and goodwill," there is **no money** exchanged. This often triggered fewer post-mortem disputes than a cash sale.
2. **Chattel Conveyance Formalities**

- Enslaved persons were legally treated as property. Deeds transferring them mirrored land deeds in every respect—complete with seals, habendum clauses, and court acknowledgments.

3. **Family Strategy & Estate Planning**

    - By transferring Seal outright, Joseph bypassed any *dower* or *heir-at-law* claims from other children upon his death. William held an in-fee estate, ensuring the girl would descend within William's branch of the family.

4. **Recordation & Notice**

    - Recording the deed at **March Term 1794** protected William against any later conflicting conveyances—vital in a frontier county where land and human property changed hands frequently.

5. **Genealogical Insights**

    - Witnesses (Waddle, Armistead, Jenkins) often were neighbors or local justices of the peace—potential leads for tracing broader family networks in Randolph County.

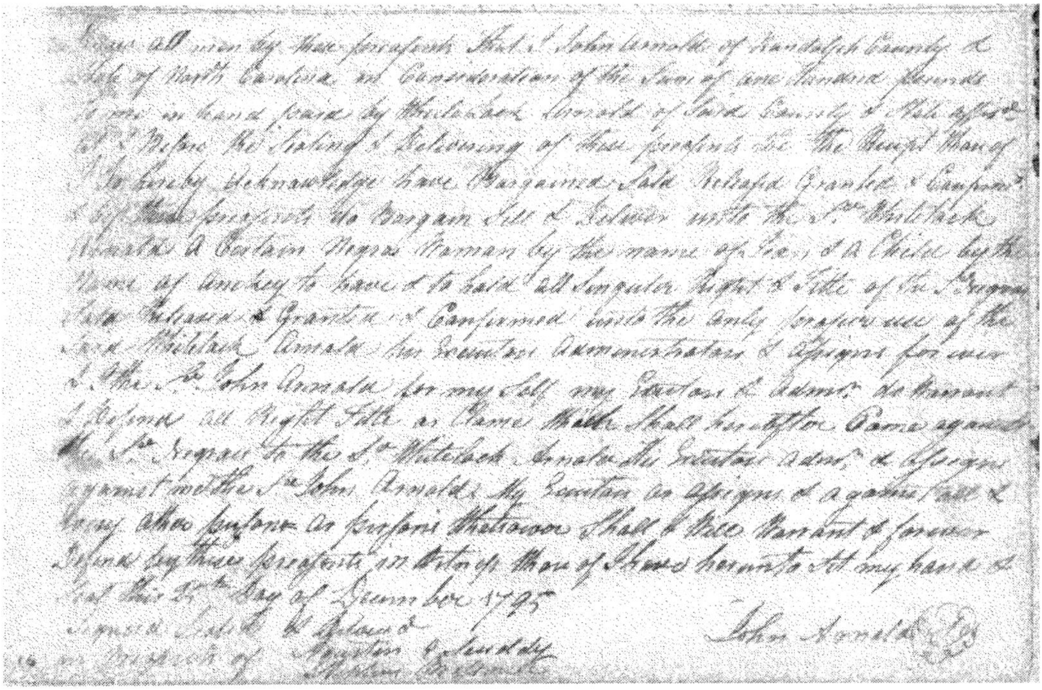
Know all men by these presents that I John Arnold of Randolph County & State of North Carolina in Consideration of the Sum of one hundred pounds to me in hand paid by Whitelock Arnold of Said County & State afores.d at & before the Sealing & delivering of these presents the Receipt whereof I do hereby acknowledge have Bargained Sold Released Granted & Confirm.d & by these presents do Bargain Sell & deliver unto the S.d Whitelock Arnold a Certain Negro Woman by the name of [illegible] & a Child by the Name of [illegible] to have & to hold all Singular Right & Title of the S.d Negroes [illegible] Released & Granted & Confirmed unto the only proper use of the Said Whitelock Arnold his Executors Administrators & Assigns for ever & I the S.d John Arnold for my Self my Executors & Admin.rs do Warrant & Defend all Right Title or Claim which Shall hereafter Come against the S.d Negroes to the S.d Whitelock Arnold his Executors Adm.rs & Assigns against me the S.d John Arnold & my Executors or Assigns & against all & every other person or persons whatsoever Shall & will Warrant & forever Defend by these presents in Witness whereof I have hereunto Set my hand & Seal this 25th Day of December 1795
Signed Sealed & Delivered in presence of [illegible] [illegible]
John Arnold (Seal)

Source location	Randolph County (NC)
Book / page	6 / 31
Record number	2
Date	December 25, 1795
Consideration	£100

Type	Bill of Sale
Grantor	John Arnold
Grantor location	Randolph
Grantee	Whitlock Arnold
Grantee location	Randolph
Abstract	Negro woman named Jean and child named Anekey
Notes	imagine being sold, with your child, on Christmas Day

Know all men by these presents that I John How of Randolph County & State of North Carolina for and in consideration of the sum of thirty seven pounds money current to me in hand paid by the said John Powell have given granted bargained and sold and by these presents do bargain grant and convey unto the said John Powell his heirs executors administrators & assigns one Negro Girl by the name of Catherine Myers a daughter of Jane a White girl To have and to hold the said Negro Girl above named with all her increase and appurtenances unto the said John Powell his heirs executors administrators and assigns for and during the natural life of the said Catherine Myers and after her decease to the said John Powell his heirs and assigns forever And I the said John How for myself my heirs executors and administrators do covenant and agree to and with the said John Powell his heirs and assigns that I am lawfully seized in fee of the premises aforesaid and have good right to sell and convey the same and that it is free from all encumbrances and that I will warrant and forever defend the same unto the said John Powell his heirs and assigns against the lawful claims of all persons whomever

In Witness Whereof I have hereunto set my hand and seal this twenty first day of January one thousand seven hundred ninety-five

(Seal)

John How

Sealed and delivered in presence of

Edmund Waddle

William Armistead

Lewis Jenkins

State of North Carolina

Randolph County } March Term 1795

The execution of the foregoing Instrument was acknowledged in open court by the said John How and ordered to be registered.

A True Copy Test: A. Harper, Clk

2. Modern-English Translation

Deed of Conveyance (January 21, 1795)

Grantor: John How (Randolph County, NC)
Grantee: John Powell (Randolph County, NC)

Consideration: £37 paid “in money current” to John How.

Property Conveyed: One enslaved female named **Catherine Myers**, daughter of another enslaved woman named **Jane** (of "white" parentage).

Estate Granted: Catherine is granted to John Powell for **her natural life**, with all offspring ("increase") and all attendant rights ("appurtenances"). **Upon Catherine's death**, full ownership of her and any issue passes **permanently** to Powell and his heirs.

Grantor's Covenants: John How warrants that

1. He **lawfully owns** Catherine in fee simple and has the right to convey her.
2. Catherine is **free of all liens or other claims**.
3. He will **defend Powell's title** and possession forever against any lawful claims.

Execution: The deed was signed, sealed, and delivered by John How on **January 21, 1795**, in the presence of three witnesses (Waddle, Armistead, Jenkins).

Court Proof & Registration: At the **March 1795** term of Randolph County court, John How personally acknowledged the deed under oath, and the court ordered it recorded.

Certification: A. Harper, Clerk, certifies this is a true copy of the registered deed.

---

3. Exhaustive Annotations

Phrase	Meaning & Effect
"Know all men by these presents"	Formal opening ("salutation") signifying the document's legal force on anyone who reads it.
"for and in consideration of the sum of thirty seven pounds money current … in hand paid"	**Consideration** clause: identifies the price (£37) paid by Powell to How, making this a **bargain and sale** rather than a mere gift. "Money current" means recognized legal tender.

"have given granted bargained and sold … and by these presents do bargain grant and convey"	Traditional string of verbs transferring full ownership interests in the property (here, an enslaved person).
"unto the said John Powell his heirs executors administrators & assigns"	Extends Powell's rights to his **heirs** (lineal descendants), **executors/administrators** (personal representatives), and **assigns** (anyone he later transfers to).
"one Negro Girl by the name of Catherine Myers a daughter of Jane a White girl"	Precisely identifies the chattel (Catherine) and her parentage (Jane). Dual naming ("Catherine Myers") covers variant spellings; parentage ties Catherine's identity in case of dispute.
"To have and to hold … for and during the natural life of the said Catherine Myers"	The **habendum clause** here grants a **life estate**: Powell holds full rights in Catherine for **her lifetime only**.
"and after her decease to the said John Powell his heirs and assigns forever"	Creates a **remainder interest**: on Catherine's death, Powell (and then his heirs) obtain **fee simple** ownership of Catherine's body and any future children she bore.
"with all her increase and appurtenances"	"Increase" = any children born to Catherine. "Appurtenances" = all rights, privileges, support, etc., that accompany her person. Ensures any issue passes to Powell.
"I … do covenant and agree … that I am lawfully seized in fee of the premises aforesaid"	**Covenant of seisin**: How affirms he truly owns Catherine in fee simple (full ownership) and can convey her.

"have good right to sell and convey the same"	**Covenant of right to convey**: How promises he has the legal authority to make this transfer.
"that it is free from all encumbrances"	**Covenant against encumbrances**: No undisclosed liens, pledges, or other claims on Catherine or her children.
"and that I will warrant and forever defend the same ... against the lawful claims of all persons whomsoever"	**Covenant of general warranty**: How guarantees Powell's ownership and will defend it against any valid claim, forever.
"In Witness Whereof I have hereunto set my hand and seal"	Marks the **formal execution**:

– **Hand**: signature or mark.
– **Seal**: wax or paper seal, still required for deeds in many jurisdictions of the 1790s. |
"Sealed and delivered in presence of [three witnesses]"	Witnesses attest that they saw How execute (sign, seal, deliver) the deed, necessary to **prove** its authenticity in court.
"March Term 1795 ... acknowledged in open court ... ordered to be registered"	At the next term of the county court, How personally **acknowledged** under oath that this was his deed, and the court ordered the clerk to **record** it in the deed books. Recording gives **constructive notice** to the world.
"A True Copy Test: A. Harper, Clk"	Certification by the clerk that this transcript is a faithful copy of the original recorded instrument. Enables reliance on the copy without inspecting the original.

Why These Elements Matter

1. **Life Estate + Remainder**

   - By granting only a life estate in Catherine (and her "increase"), How retains nothing after her death; at that point, Powell's heirs hold full title. This split estate structure—life tenant (Powell) vs. remainderman (also Powell & his heirs)—was common to control succession of enslaved property.

2. **Covenants of Title**
    - The four present covenants (seisin, right to convey, freedom from encumbrances, warranty) give Powell maximum protection. If any defect arises—say, a prior lien—Powell can sue How (or his estate).
3. **Parentage & Naming**
    - Recording Catherine's mother ("Jane a White girl") and Catherine's own surname prevents identity disputes—especially important where record-keeping and slave births were inconsistently documented.
4. **Recording & Notice**
    - Once registered at "March Term 1795," any subsequent purchaser or creditor in Randolph County would be on notice of Powell's life estate and remainder interest, defeating later competing claims.
5. **Clerk's Certification**
    - The "True Copy" endorsement allows lawyers, surveyors, and descendants to rely on this copy as if it were the original entry in the deed books.

Know all men by these that I Ephraim Andrews of the County of Randolph & State of North
Carolina for & in Consideration of the Sum of Sixty pounds Current Money of the County
& State [illegible] to me in hand paid at & before the Sealing & Delivering of these
presents by Ephraim Andrews the receipt whereof I do hereby Acknowledge have bargained
& Sold & by these presents do bargain & Sell unto the Sd. John Harvey one Negro fellow
Name Arthur & by these presents Bargained Sold unto John Harvey his Exrs. Admrs.
& Assigns forever & I the Sd. Ephraim Andrews for my Self my Exrs. & Admrs. all &
Singular the Sd. Negro fellow unto the Sd. John Harvey his Exrs. Admrs. & Assigns
against me the Sd. Ephraim Andrews my Exrs. Admrs. & Assigns & Against all &
every other person & persons whatever Shall & Will Warrant & forever Defend by
these presents of Which Negro I the Sd. Andrews [illegible] put the Sd. Harvey in full
possession by Delivering him the Sd. Negro at the Sealing hereof In Witness

September 17th day 1794

Jeremiah Cox Jurat

Isaac Webb

Ephraim Andrews (Seal)

State No. Carolina } Randolph County } February Term 1795

The Execution of the above Bill of Sale was duly
Proven in open Court by Jeremiah Cox & Ordered to be Registered

A True Copy Test

[illegible] Harper Clk

Source location	Randolph County (NC)
Book / page	6 / 49
Record number	2
Date	September 17, 1794
Consideration	£60

Type	Bill of Sale
Grantor	Ephraim Andrews
Grantor location	Randolph
Grantee	John Harvey
Grantee location	Randolph
Abstract	Negro fellow named [Potter?] sold by Ephraim Andrews to John Harvey for £60

Know all men by these presents that I William Sanders of the County of Randolph & State of North Carolina for and in consideration of the sum of thirty seven pounds money current to me in hand paid & before the delivering of these presents by John Craven Clerk of the County aforesaid have bargained and sold and by these presents do bargain grant and convey unto the said James Simmons the straight black Jane & her future increase & appurtenances to the said James Simmons his heirs and assigns forever the said Negro Jane with her future increase & appurtenances to be equally disposed of by delivering him the said Negro at the making hereof this 19th day of September 1794

(Seal)

Wm Sanders

Sealed and delivered in presence of

James Reid

John Webb

State of North Carolina

Randolph County } February Term 1795

The execution of the above deed by said Wm Sanders

was upon oath proved by James Reid & John Webb witnesses

to be the act and deed of the said Sanders & ordered to be registered.

A True Copy Test: A. Harper, Clk

2. Modern-English Translation

Be it known to everyone:
I, **William Sanders** of Randolph County, North Carolina, have received **£37** (in lawful money) in hand from **James Simmons**, before delivering this deed. In return I now **bargain, grant, and convey** to James Simmons, his heirs, and assigns **forever**

- **One enslaved woman**, named **Jane** (described as "the straight black Jane"),
- **All of Jane's future offspring** ("increase"),
- **All attendant rights** ("appurtenances").

I deliver Jane to James Simmons **right now**, on **September 19, 1794**.

Witnesses: James Reid; John Webb.

Court Proof: At the February 1795 term of Randolph County court, Reid and Webb swore that William Sanders himself made and signed this deed. The court thereupon ordered it recorded.

Certification: A. Harper, Clerk, certifies this is a true copy of the recorded instrument.

---

3. Exhaustive Annotations

Phrase	Meaning & Legal Effect
"Know all men by these presents"	Formal opening ("salutation") indicating the deed's binding force on anyone who reads it.
"I William Sanders of the County of Randolph & State of North Carolina"	Identifies the **grantor** and his residence for jurisdictional clarity.
"for and in consideration of the sum of thirty seven pounds money current to me in hand paid"	**Consideration clause**: £37 was paid by the grantee, making this a bona fide **sale** (not a gift). "Money current" = recognized legal tender.
"& before the delivering of these presents by John Craven Clerk of the County aforesaid"	Indicates the payment was made **before** the deed was delivered; names the county clerk who first held the document for record.
"have bargained and sold and by these presents do bargain grant and convey"	Traditional string of conveyance verbs:

– **Bargain and sell** (the core sale language)
– **Grant** (formal transfer)
– **Convey** (to pass title) |
"unto the said James Simmons his heirs and assigns forever"	Grants a **fee simple absolute** to Simmons and his successors in perpetuity.
"the straight black Jane"	Identifies the enslaved person as "Jane" and describes her appearance or lineage ("straight black"). Precision avoids identity disputes.
"& her future increase"	"Increase" = any children born to Jane. These too pass to Simmons.
"& appurtenances"	"Appurtenances" = all rights and benefits that accompany Jane as property.
"to be equally disposed of"	Clarifies that Jane's future children are to be distributed among Simmons's heirs in equal shares (common phrasing when dividing increase).
"by delivering him the said Negro at the making hereof"	**Delivery clause**: physical transfer of Jane to Simmons occurs immediately upon signing.
"this 19th day of September 1794"	The **execution date**, which fixes priority against later claims.
"(Seal) Wm Sanders"	**Signature & seal**: Sanders's mark and seal make the deed formally binding.
"Sealed and delivered in presence of [witnesses]"	Witness attestations that Sanders executed (signed, sealed, delivered) the deed—required for later proof.
"February Term 1795 … acknowledged in open court … ordered to be registered"	At the next county-court session, the grantor personally **acknowledged** the deed under oath; the court then **ordered** the clerk to enter it in the deed books, giving **constructive notice** to all.
"A True Copy Test: A. Harper, Clk"	The clerk's certification that this transcript exactly matches the original recorded deed, so it can be used as authoritative evidence.

Why These Elements Matter

1. **Full Fee Simple**

    ○ By conveying "forever… unto his heirs and assigns," Sanders gives Simmons the most complete estate in Jane and her increase.

2. **Consideration & Delivery**

- The explicit payment of £37 and immediate delivery ensure no ambiguities about value exchanged or Sanders's intent.

3. **Increase & Equal Disposition**

    - "Increase" language bundled future children into the grant. The equal-disposition clause clarifies how those children are later divided among Simmons's heirs.

4. **Witnesses & Court Acknowledgment**

    - Witness signatures plus a formal court acknowledgement under oath protect against any later claims that Sanders lacked capacity or that the deed was forged.

5. **Recording**

    - Once "ordered to be registered," this deed became part of the public record, defeating any subsequent grantor or creditor claims against Jane or her future children.

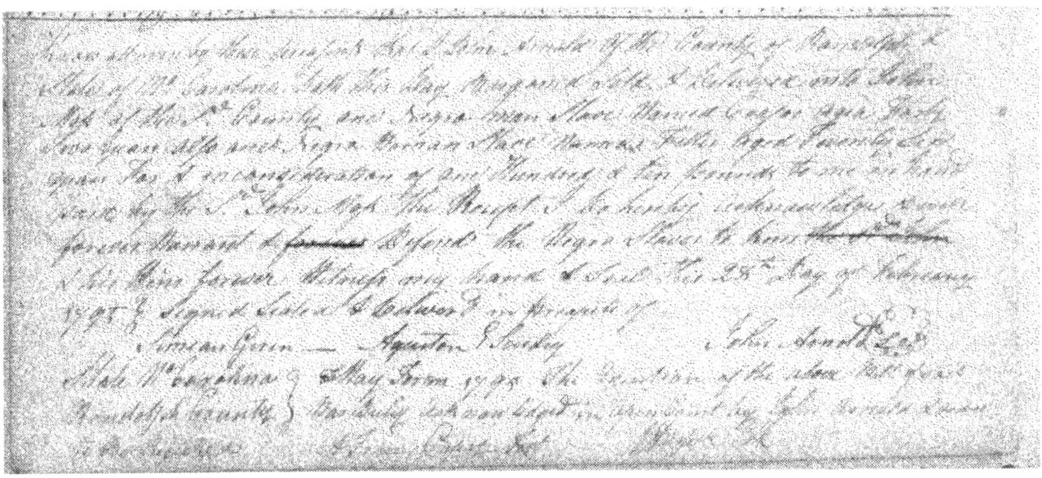

September 19th day 1794

Sealed & delivered in presence of

James Reid

John Webb

State of North Carolina

Randolph County } February Term 1795

The execution of the above deed by said Wm Sanders

was upon oath proved by James Reid & John Webb witnesses

to be the act and deed of the said Sanders & ordered to be registered.

A True Copy Test: A. Harper, Clk

2. Modern-English Translation

- **Date:** September 19, 1794
- **Execution:** William Sanders "sealed and delivered" the deed in the presence of two witnesses—**James Reid** and **John Webb**.
- **Court Acknowledgment (Feb. 1795):** At the February term of the Randolph County court, Reid and Webb swore under oath that they had seen Sanders sign and deliver the deed. The court thereupon ordered the deed to be recorded in the county deed book.
- **Clerk's Certification:** A. Harper, Clerk of Court, certifies that this page is a true copy of the recorded instrument.

---

3. Brief Annotations

- **"Sealed & delivered"**: Confirms formal execution (signature + seal + transfer).
- **Witness names**: Provide proof that Sanders had at least two disinterested witnesses—necessary for later validation.

- **Court proof ("upon oath proved…ordered to be registered")**: Sanders's deed was formally **acknowledged** in open court, meeting statutory requirements for recordation.

- **"A True Copy Test"**: The clerk's attestation that this transcription exactly matches the original deed as entered in the public records.

his Heirs & Assigns from time to time & at all times hereafter Peaceably & Quietly [illegible] hold possess & Enjoy the sd. Messuage & all & singular other the premises [illegible] Mentioned & Intended to be hereby Granted with their Appurtenances without any Lawfull Let Suit Trouble or Interruption of him the sd. William Field Junr. his Heirs or Assigns or any other person whatsoever the Lands or Lessors [illegible] the Premises to the Hereby Granted & Confirmed & the sd. William Field Junr. his Heirs Exrs. & Admrs. doeth Covenant & Grant to & with the Wm. Field Senr. by these presents that shall & may be Lawfull to & for the sd. Wm. Field Junr. his Heirs & Assigns from time to time & at all times forever hereafter Peaceably & Quietly to have hold possess & Enjoy the sd. Messuage & premises with their Appurtenances without the Lawfull Let Suit Trouble or Interruption of him the sd. William Field Senr. or Mary his Wife his Heirs Exrs. Admrs. or any of them or any other person or persons Lawfully claiming to Claim in by from or under him or them or any of them the Wm. Field Senr. his Heirs Exrs. & Admrs. & Covenant & Grant to & with the sd. William Field Junr. his Heirs & Assigns by these presents that the the sd. Wm. Field Senr. his Heirs shall & will at any time or times hereafter upon the Request & at the proper Cost & Charges in the Law of the sd. Wm. Field Junr. his Heirs or Assigns [illegible] Make & Execute or Cause & procure to be Made Done & Executed All & Every such further & other Deeds Conveyances or Assurances in the Law Whatsoever for the further better Conveying & Assuring the sd. Messuage & premises with their Appurtenances unto the sd. Wm. Field Senr. his Heirs to the use of the sd. William Field Junr. his Heirs [illegible] by any [illegible] Releases or Conveyances [illegible] only the sd. William Field [illegible] [illegible] shall be Reasonably Devised Advised or Required [illegible] further Assurance [illegible] further Covenant or [illegible] in these presents Contain. In Witness whereof the sd. William Field Junr. hath hereunto set his hand & fixed his seal

State of No. Carolina }
Randolph County } November Term 1795

The Execution of this Deed of Conveyance was duly [illegible] [illegible] [illegible] William Field Junr. [illegible] Ordered to be [illegible]

A Copy Test. [illegible] Clerk

State of No. Carolina
Randolph County [illegible]

Know all men by these presents that I [illegible]

The Execution of this [illegible] [illegible] [illegible] [illegible] [illegible] Clerk

Know all men by these presents that I Alexander Threpect of Randolph County & State of North Carolina for and in consideration of the sum of one hundred & eighty dollars to me in hand paid by William Fletcher have bargained and sold & do hereby bargain grant and convey unto the said William Fletcher one negro girl named Jane a mulatto child daughter of Jane a white girl and her future increase and appurtenances to the said William Fletcher his heirs executors administrators and assigns forever. And I the said Alexander Threpect for myself my heirs executors and administrators do covenant with the said William Fletcher his heirs executors administrators and assigns that I am lawfully seized in fee of the said negro girl and her future increase and that the same is free from all encumbrances and that I will warrant and forever defend the said negro girl and her future increase unto the said William Fletcher his heirs executors administrators and assigns against the lawful claims of all persons whatso-ever.

In witness whereof I have hereunto set my hand and seal this fourteenth day of June 1795.

(Seal)

Alexander Threpect (his X mark)

Sealed and delivered in presence of

John Craven

James Logan

State of North Carolina

Randolph County } November Term 1795

The execution of the above deed by said Alexander Threpect was proved in open court by John Craven and James Logan his witnesses to be his act and deed and ordered to be registered.

A True Copy Test: A. Harper, Clk

2. Modern-English Translation

Deed of Sale (June 14, 1795)

I, **Alexander Threpect** of Randolph County, NC, for **$180** paid by **William Fletcher**, hereby sell and convey to William Fletcher (and to Fletcher's heirs, executors, administrators, and assigns) **one enslaved mulatto girl named Jane**, daughter of an enslaved woman named Jane (described as "a white girl"), **together with any children she may have in the future** ("increase"), and **all attendant rights** ("appurtenances").

I warrant that:

1. I own Jane and her future children in fee simple ("I am lawfully seized in fee").

2. No liens or other claims burden her ("free from all encumbrances").

3. I will defend Fletcher's title forever against any lawful claim.

Executed (signed and sealed) June 14, 1795, in the presence of witnesses **John Craven** and **James Logan**.

Court Proof (Nov. Term 1795): Craven and Logan swore in open court that they saw Threpect execute the deed; the court thereupon ordered it recorded.

Clerk's Certification: A. Harper, Clerk of Randolph County, certifies this is a true copy of the recorded instrument.

---

3. Key Points

- **Consideration ($180):** A clear cash payment distinguishes this from a "love and affection" gift.
- **Immediate Delivery:** Jane was turned over to Fletcher "at the sealing and delivering" of the deed.
- **Fee Simple & Warranty:** Threpect grants the highest form of ownership, promising to defend Fletcher's title "against the lawful claims of all persons whatsoever."
- **"Increase & Appurtenances":** Any children Jane bore automatically passed to Fletcher under this deed.
- **Court Acknowledgment & Recordation:** Formal proof in court (the "acknowledgment") was necessary under 18th-century NC law before a deed could be recorded and binding on third parties.
- **Clerk's "True Copy Test":** Allows anyone to rely on this transcript as if reading the original deed in the bound county records.

& Interest [illegible] the s^d Mary [illegible] her heirs [illegible] the heirs & assigns shall [illegible] persons Claiming by from or under him or them & also from & against all & all Manner of persons Whatsoever lawfully Claiming or to Claim the s^d [illegible] premises or any part or parcel [illegible] thereof & further that [illegible] at any time hereafter at the [illegible] Request & Charges of the s^d John Barton his heirs or assigns Make do [illegible] & Deliver All Such further & other [illegible] Deeds thing & things [illegible] Conveyances & assurances in the Law for the better & more [illegible] [illegible] of the s^d John [illegible] [illegible] or assigns of in & to the afs^d [illegible] premises [illegible] by him or them or any of them or his or their Counsel [illegible] the same shall be reasonably advised [illegible] or Required In Witness Whereof the s^d Mary [illegible] McCulloch hath hereunto set her hand & Seal of arms the day & year first above Written

Signed & Sealed the day & year within [illegible] & [illegible] the within [illegible] [illegible] the s^d sum of 315 [illegible] the [illegible] Money within [illegible] to be paid to me — 315 : 0 : 0

Mary [illegible] McCulloch

Mary [illegible] McCulloch

[illegible]

[illegible] County } November Term 1794

The [illegible] of the foregoing Deed of Conveyance [illegible] [illegible] [illegible]

A True Copy [illegible] — [illegible] Clk

Know all Men by these presents that I John Clark of [illegible] County [illegible] [illegible] of the sum of forty pounds to me in hand paid by [illegible] [illegible] [illegible] [illegible] the Receipt whereof I do hereby acknowledge [illegible] by these presents [illegible] Grant Bargain & Sell unto the s^d [illegible] [illegible] [illegible] by the Name of [illegible] to have & to hold the s^d [illegible] by these presents [illegible] [illegible] & Grant unto the only proper use & behoof of the s^d [illegible] [illegible] & assigns forever & I the s^d John Clark for my heirs [illegible] [illegible] the s^d [illegible] to the s^d [illegible] [illegible] & assigns [illegible] [illegible] & against all & every other person & persons Whatsoever [illegible] [illegible] these presents In Witness Whereof I the s^d John Clark have hereunto set my hand & Seal the [illegible] day of September 1794

[illegible] County [illegible] Term 1794

[illegible]

[illegible] Clk

1. Transcription

...and warrant and forever defend the said negro girl and her future increase unto the said William Fletcher his heirs executors administrators and assigns against the lawful claims of all persons whatso-ever.
And I the said Alexander Threpert for myself my heirs executors and administrators do covenant with the said William Fletcher his heirs executors administrators and assigns that I will warrant and forever defend the said negro girl and her future increase unto the said William Fletcher his heirs executors administrators and assigns against the lawful claims of all persons whatso-ever.

In witness whereof I have hereunto set my hand and seal this fourteenth day of June 1795.

(Seal)
Alexander Threpert (his X mark)

Sealed and delivered in presence of

John Craven
James Logan

State of North Carolina
Randolph County } November Term 1795
The execution of the above deed by said Alexander Threpert was proved in open court by John Craven and James Logan his witnesses to be his act and deed and ordered to be registered.

A True Copy Test: A. Harper, Clk

Received the day & year within written
of the above consideration thirty five pounds to me in hand paid by William Fletcher I have paid the above named negro girls and delivered her into the possession of the said William Fletcher.

Thos P. McClelland

State of North Carolina
Randolph County } November Term 1795
The execution of the foregoing recital was duly proved in open court by John Craven & James Logan to be the act and deed of the said Alexander Threpert.

A True Copy Test: A. Harper, Clk

2. Modern-English Translation

Warrant & Defense
I, Alexander Threpert, fully guarantee that the enslaved girl (and any children she may bear) now conveyed to William Fletcher—along with all attendant rights—shall be free of all claims. I promise to defend Fletcher's ownership against any lawful challenge by anyone.

Execution
Signed, sealed, and delivered by Alexander Threpert (his "X" mark) on June 14, 1795, in the presence of John Craven and James Logan.

Court Acknowledgment (Nov. Term 1795)
In Randolph County's November 1795 court session, Craven and Logan swore that Threpert personally executed the deed; the court then ordered it recorded.

Receipt of Part Payment
I acknowledge receipt of **£35** from William Fletcher, and confirm I have turned the aforementioned enslaved girls over to Fletcher's possession.

Second Court Proof & Registration
At the same November 1795 term, Craven and Logan again proved (by oath) that this recital is Threpert's act, and the court ordered it recorded.

Clerk's Certification
A. Harper, Clerk, certifies this is a true copy of the deed as entered in the records.

---

3. Notes on Key Phrases

- **"Warrant and forever defend"**: A **covenant of warranty**, promising Threpert will safeguard Fletcher's clear title against any lawful claims.
- **"Future increase"**: Any children born to the enslaved girl automatically transferred to Fletcher.
- **Witness & court acknowledgment**: Nineteenth-century North Carolina required two witnesses plus a court acknowledgment ("proved in open court") before a deed could be recorded.
- **Receipt clause**: Confirms that £35 of the purchase price was paid and that the enslaved girl was delivered to Fletcher. This separate receipt (by Thos P. McClelland) was

sometimes used when payment and delivery occurred after the deed's signing.

- **"A True Copy Test"**: The clerk's attestation that this is a faithful transcript of the original, fully recorded deed.

the Thomas King hath hereunto set his hand & seal the day and year above written

State of North Carolina } February Term 1797

Randolph County } the Execution of the above Deed of conveyance was Duly Proved in Open Court by John Spencer & ordered to be Registered.

Copy Test H Harper Clerk

Know all men by these presents that I Simeon Green of Randolph County for & in consideration of the Sum of one Hundred pounds to him in hand paid by John McDaniel of said County at & before the Sealing & Delivering of these presents the Receipt whereof is hereby acknowledged have Bargained & Sold & by these presents doth grant & sell unto the said John McDaniel one negroe woman Slave by the name of Betty to have & to hold the said Slave & all her further Increase by these presents Bargained & Sold granted unto the only proper use & behoof of the said John McDaniel his heirs Executors & Administrators & assigns forever & the said Simeon Green to warrant the said Slave to be a sound well healthy wench at this time for myself my heirs Executors & Administrators & singular the said Slave twenty years of age unto the said John McDaniel his heirs & assigns against me the said Simeon Green my heirs & assigns & against all every other person or persons whatsoever will warrant & forever defend by these presents in Witness whereof I the said Simeon Green have hereunto set my hand & Seal this Eighteenth Day of October 1796

State of North Carolina } February Term 1797

Randolph County } the Execution of the within Bill of Sale from Simeon Green to John McDaniel was Duly acknowledged in open Court by Simeon Green & ordered to be Registered

Copy Test H Harper Clerk

Source location	Randolph County (NC)
Book / page	7 / 79
Date	October 18, 1796
Consideration	£100
Type	Bill of Sale
Grantor	Simeon Geron
Grantee	John McDaniel
Abstract	woman named Betty, 20, and all her "further increase". Grantor appears to be the Sheriff of Randolph County at the time, but the slave was apparently sold in his personal capacity

Know all men by these presents that I Simon Green of Randolph County for and in consideration of the sum of one hundred pounds to me in hand paid by John W. Daniel of said County at and before the sealing & delivery of these presents the receipt whereof is hereby acknowledged, hath bargained & sold & by these presents doth grant & sell unto the said John W. Daniel one negro woman slave by the name of Patsy a mulatto child of Jane a white woman & her future increase by these presents bargained & sold & granted unto the said John W. Daniel his heirs, executors, administrators & assigns forever; to have & to hold the said slave & her future increase unto the said John W. Daniel his heirs & assigns; and I the said Simon Green for myself, my heirs, executors & administrators do covenant to and with the said John W. Daniel his heirs, executors, administrators & assigns that I will warrant the said slave to be a sound, well and healthy creature at the time of sale, that I have good right and lawful authority to sell & convey the same, and that I will warrant & forever defend the said slave & her future increase to be the property of the said John W. Daniel his heirs & assigns against the lawful claims of all persons whomsoever.

In witness whereof I the said Simon Green have hereunto set my hand and seal this eighteenth day of October 1796.

(Seal)

Simon Green (his X mark)

Sealed and delivered in presence of

John Craven

James Logan

State of North Carolina

Randolph County } February Term 1797

The execution of the within Deed of sale from Simon Green to John W. Daniel was duly acknowledged in open court by Simon Green & ordered to be registered.

A true Copy Test: A. Harper, Clk

2. Modern-English Translation

Deed of Sale (October 18, 1796)

I, **Simon Green** of Randolph County, North Carolina, for **£100** paid in full by **John W. Daniel**, hereby sell and convey to John W. Daniel (and to his heirs, executors, administrators, and assigns) **one enslaved mulatto woman named Patsy**, daughter of an enslaved woman named Jane (described as “a white woman”), **together with any children she may have in the future** (“her future increase”).

I warrant that Patsy is a **sound, well, and healthy** person at the time of sale; that I legally own her; that I have full right and authority to sell her; and that I will **defend** Daniel’s ownership forever against any lawful claim by anyone.

Executed (signed, sealed, delivered) October 18, 1796, in the presence of **John Craven** and **James Logan**.

Court Acknowledgment (Feb. Term 1797): In Randolph County’s February 1797 court session, Simon Green swore this deed is his act and deed; the court then ordered it recorded.

Clerk’s Certification: A. Harper, Clerk, certifies this is a true copy of the recorded deed.

3. Notes on Key Clauses

- **"For and in consideration of … £100 … paid …"**
  Establishes the sale price and that payment was made **before** the deed's delivery.

- **"Bargained & sold … grant & sell"**
  Traditional legal formulas covering every aspect of transferring title.

- **"One negro woman slave … and her future increase"**
  Patsy and any children she may bear are included in the transfer.

- **"To have & to hold … forever"**
  The **habendum** clause granting a fee-simple estate with full inheritability.

- **"I will warrant the said slave … free from all encumbrances … and forever defend"**
  A **general warranty** of title, promising to protect Daniel's ownership against any lawful challenges.

- **Witnesses & court acknowledgment**
  Two witnesses plus a formal acknowledgment in open court were required under 1790s North Carolina law to make the deed recordable and binding on third parties.

- **"A true Copy Test"**
  The clerk's attestation that this transcript matches the original entry in the deed books, so it can be relied on without inspecting the bound volume.

Yearly or otherwise as the General Assembly Shall direct & the said Samuel for himself & his heirs &c against him the Samuel Aiken his heirs Exec^rs & admin^rs all other persons whatsoever Lawfully Claiming any part of the said granted Lands or premises to the said Conrad Jones his heirs & assigns forever Defend by the presents in Witness Whereof the said Samuel Aiken hath set his hand & Seal the Day & year above Written

State of North Carolina } February Term 1777
Randolph County } the Execution of the above deed was duly Proven in Open Court by William Williams & ordered to be Registered

Copy Test Harper Clerk

Know all Men by these Presents that I James & Susa Hutton of the County of Randolph of Chatham & State of North Carolina for & in consideration of the Sum of Eighty five Pounds to us in hand paid by John Coble of Randolph County & State aforesaid the Receipt whereof we doth hereby acknowledge have Bargained & Sold Delivered & by these Presents doth grant Bargain & Deliver in Plain & Open Market unto the said John Coble his heirs Executors & Administrators a Certain Negroe woman named Easter to have & to hold the said Bargained woman unto the said John Coble his heirs Exec^rs & Adm^rs & Assigns forever & we the said James & Susa Hutton for our Selves & our heirs Exec^rs Admin^rs Shall & will warrant & forever Defend the above Described Negroe woman unto the said John Coble his heirs Exec^rs Adm^rs in witness whereof we have hereunto set our hands & affixed our Seals twenty first day of November 1796

State of North Carolina } February Term 1777
Randolph County } the Execution of the above bill of sale was Duly Proved in Open Court by John Coble & ordered to be Registered

Copy Test Harper Clerk

Source location	Randolph County (NC)
Book / page	7 / 94
Date	November 21, 1796
Consideration	£85
Type	Bill of Sale
Grantor	James and Susa Hutton
Grantee	John Coble
Abstract	Negro woman. Grantors are of Chatham County.

Know all men by these presents that I James & Lisa Holton of the County of Randolph & State of North Carolina for and in consideration of the sum of eighty four pounds to us in hand paid by John Cable of Randolph County & State aforesaid the receipt whereof we do hereby acknowledge have bargained & sold & delivered & by these presents do bargain & sell

& deliver in fee simple to the said John Cable his heirs executors & administrators & assigns a certain negro woman named Carter to have & to hold the said bargained & sold & conveyed forever unto the said John Cable his heirs executors administrators & assigns forever and we the said James & Lisa Holton for ourselves our heirs executors & administrators do covenant & promise & agree to and with the said John Cable his heirs & assigns that he shall & may peaceably & quietly enjoy the said negro woman unto the said John Cable his heirs executors administrators & assigns against the claim or claims of all persons whatsoever & we will warrant & forever defend the said negro woman unto the said John Cable his heirs & assigns.

In witness whereof we have hereunto set our hands & affixed our seals this twenty first day of November 1796.

(Seal)

James Holton

Lisa Holton (her X mark)

Sealed and delivered in presence of

John Craven

James Logan

State of North Carolina

Randolph County } November Term 1796

The execution of the above Bill of Sale was duly proved in open court

by John Craven & James Logan & ordered to be registered.

A True Copy Test: A. Harper, Clk

2. Modern-English Translation

Deed of Sale (Nov. 21, 1796)

We, **James Holton** and **Lisa Holton** of Randolph County, North Carolina, for **£84** paid in full by **John Cable**, hereby sell, transfer, and deliver to John Cable (and to his heirs, executors, administrators, and assigns) **one enslaved woman named Carter**, to have and to hold in **fee simple**—absolute ownership—**forever**.

We further covenant that John Cable shall **peaceably and quietly** possess Carter, free from any claims by us or anyone claiming through us, and we will **warrant and forever defend** his title to her against all lawful claims.

Executed (signed, sealed, delivered) on November 21, 1796, in the presence of **John Craven** and **James Logan**.

Court Proof & Registration (Nov. Term 1796): Craven and Logan swore in open court that they witnessed the Holtons execute this bill of sale, and the court thereupon ordered it recorded.

Clerk's Certificate: A. Harper certifies this is a true copy of the recorded instrument.

---

3. Detailed Annotations

Phrase	Purpose & Legal Effect

“Know all men by these presents”	Standard **salutation** declaring the deed’s binding nature on anyone who reads it.
“for and in consideration of the sum of eighty four pounds … paid by John Cable … the receipt whereof we do hereby acknowledge”	**Consideration clause:** shows a cash sale for £84, fully paid prior to delivery. “Receipt … acknowledge” prevents later disputes about payment.
“have bargained & sold & delivered & by these presents do bargain & sell & deliver”	Traditional **conveyancing verbs** ensuring the grant is effective.
“in fee simple”	Grants **absolute ownership**, unrestricted in duration or heirship.
“to the said John Cable his heirs executors & administrators & assigns forever”	Extends the estate to Cable’s **heirs**, **personal representatives**, and **anyone he later transfers to**, in perpetuity.
“a certain negro woman named Carter”	Identifies the enslaved person by name; specificity avoids confusion.
“to have & to hold … forever”	The **habendum clause**, defining the **extent** (entire interest) and **duration** (forever) of the grant.
“covenant & promise … that he shall & may peaceably & quietly enjoy”	**Quiet enjoyment covenant:** Cable will not be disturbed in his possession by the grantors or their successors.

"we will warrant & forever defend the said negro woman … against the claim or claims of all persons whatsoever"	**General warranty covenant:** the Holtons guarantee Cable's clear title and promise to defend it against any lawful challenges.
"In witness whereof we have hereunto set our hands & affixed our seals"	**Execution clause:** signatures (or marks) plus seals make the deed formally binding.
Witnesses	John Craven and James Logan attest to the Holtons' execution, necessary for proof in court.
Court Acknowledgment ("proved in open court … ordered to be registered")	Formal **acknowledgment** under oath, required in 1790s North Carolina for a deed to be recorded—giving **constructive notice** to all third parties.
"A True Copy Test"	Clerk's attestation that this transcript matches the original deed book entry, so it can be relied on as authoritative.

Why it matters:

- **Fee simple + warranty covenants** provide Cable the highest level of protection: he owns Carter outright, can pass her to his heirs, and no one can lawfully contest that title.
- **Peaceable possession** promises he won't be ousted by rival claimants.
- **Recordation** at court term ensures everyone in Randolph County is on notice of his ownership.

242 Know all men by these presents that I Charles Parish of the City of Raleigh State of N^o Carolina for & in consideration of the Sum of 225 Spanish Milled Dollars to me in hand paid by Thomas Mathews of the County of Randolph & State aff^d. the Receipt Whereof I do acknowledge hath Granted Bargained & Sold & by these Presents doath grant Bargain & Sell & Deliver unto the S^d Thomas Mathews his heirs &c, forever a Negro Girl Slave aged about Ten years & her future Increase named Betsey, Wherefore I do Warrant & forever defend, the Right and title of the aff^d Negro Girl Slave her further Increase unto him the S^d Mathews to his Heirs & assigns forever, & against the Claims of My Self My Heirs, &c, or any person or persons Whatsoever In Witness Whereof I have hereto Set my hand this 7th Day of March 1801

State of N^o Carolina }
Randolph County } May Term 1801

The Execution of the above bill of Sale was duly Proved in open Court by Thomas Watson & ordered to be Registered. Copy Test Harper Clk

487

This Indenture Made the 3^d day of December in the year 1800 Between Ebenezer Snow of the County of Randolph State of N^o Carolina, of the one part & Thomas Beard of the County & State aff^d of the other part Witnesseth that the S^d Ebenezer Snow for & in consideration of the Sum of 380 Dollars in hand the Receipt Whereof is hereby Acknowledged hath Granted Bargained & Sold & by these Presents doath Grant Bargain & Sell Aliens Confirm unto the S^d Thomas Beard his Heirs & assigns a Certain piece or Tract of Land lying in Randolph County on the Waters of Caraway the Plantation Wm Snow now lives on Beg^g at a White oak, & Running South 133½ poles to Thomas Andrews Corner, Red oak, then then West 180 poles to a Stake, on the Creek, then North 133½ poles to a pine then East 180 poles to a White oak the Beginning Corner, containing 150 Acres be the Same More or Less Together With all Mines Minerals Woods Waters Ways Commodities and advantages & appurtenances Whatsoever to the S^d Messuage Belonging or in any wise Appertaining & also the Reversion & Reversions Remainder & Remainders Rents & Services of the S^d Premises & of every Part thereof & all the Estate Right Title Interest Claim & Demand Whatsoever of him the S^d Ebenezer Snow of in & to the S^d Messuage piece or parcel of Land & every Part thereof To Have & To Hold, the S^d Messuage or piece of Land, & every part thereof With the appurtenances unto the S^d Thomas Beard his Heirs & assigns to the only proper use & Behoof of him the S^d Thomas Beard his Heirs & assigns forever & he the S^d Ebenezer Snow for himself & his Heirs the S^d Messuage & Premises aff^d against himself & his heirs & against all & every other Person or Persons to the S^d Thomas Beard his Heirs & assigns Shall Warrant & forever Defend by these Presents in Witness Whereof the S^d Ebenezer Snow hath hereto Set his hand & affixed his Seal the Day & year above Written —

State of North Carolina }
Randolph County — } May Term 1801

the Execution of the Within Deed of Conveyance was Duly Proved in open Court by John Beard ~~& ordered~~ & one of the Subscribing Witnesses & ordered to be Registered
Copy Test Harper Clk

488

N° 58 This Indenture Made the 16th Day of September Anno. Dom, 1790 Between Jonathan Harper Jesse Henley Samuel Millikan William Bell & Zebedee Wood Esq^rs Commissioners & Trustees of the Town of Johnston Ville in the County of Randolph & State of N^o Carolina of the one Part & Robert Anderson of the County of Randolph of the other part Whereas By Virtue of an Act of the General Assembly passed at Fayette Ville the Sixth Day of December Anno. Dom, 1788, Intitled an Act for erecting ~~for~~ a Town on the Lands of Thomas Dougan, in Randolph County the S^d Jonathan Harper Jesse Henley Samuel Millikan William Bell & Zebedee Wood Esq^rs are Legally & Duly appointed Commissioners

Source location	Randolph County (NC)
Book / page	8 / 242
Date	March 7, 1804
Consideration	225 Spanish Mill dollars
Type	Bill of Sale
Grantor	Charles Parish
Grantee	Thomas Matthews
Abstract	Negro girl slave named Betsey, about 10

No. 242 Bill of Sale of a Negro Girl (7 Mar 1801 & proved May 1801)

1. Diplomatic Transcription

242

Know all men by these presents that I, **Charles Parish** of the city of **Raleigh**, state of **North Carolina**, for and in consideration of the sum of **two hundred and twenty pounds specie** to me in hand paid by **Thomas Matthews** of the county of **Randolph** & state aforesaid (the receipt whereof I do acknowledge),
hath granted, bargained, sold, and by these presents doth grant, bargain, sell and deliver unto the said Thomas Matthews, his heirs & assigns, **one negro girl slave, aged about thirteen years**, to have and to hold the said negro girl slave, her future increase, unto him the said Matthews, his heirs & assigns for ever, **and against the claims of myself, my heirs, executors or administrators, or any person or persons whatsoever**.

In witness whereof I have hereunto set my hand this **7□h day of March 1801**.

(Seal) Charles Parish

State of North Carolina, Randolph County
Court of Pleas & Quarter Sessions, May Term 1801
The execution of the above bill of sale was duly proved in open court by Thomas Wilson & ordered to be registered.
Copy Test A. Harper, Clk.

2. Modern-English Rendering

Sale of a 13-year-old enslaved girl (March 7 1801)

I, **Charles Parish** of Raleigh, NC, in return for **£220 in specie** paid by **Thomas Matthews** of Randolph County, hereby sell and transfer to him (and to his heirs and assigns forever) a **13-year-old enslaved girl**. I warrant that I lawfully own her and that no one else has any claim against her.

Executed March 7 1801. At the May 1801 term, the Randolph County court heard testimony (by Thomas Wilson) and ordered this bill of sale recorded.

3. Clause-by-Clause Notes

Phrase	**Effect & Purpose**
"consideration of … £220 specie"	Records the exact **sale price** and that payment was in coin, eliminating later disputes.
"granted, bargained, sold … doth grant, bargain, sell and deliver"	A full set of **conveyance verbs** leaving no doubt a transfer of ownership has occurred.
"unto the said Thomas Matthews, his heirs & assigns for ever"	Grants a **perpetual** right of ownership, including to Matthew's descendants or transferees.
"one negro girl slave, aged about thirteen years"	Names the enslaved person (though without

a given name) and fixes her age for identification. |
"her future increase"	Conveys any children she may bear, ensuring Matthew acquires her entire family line.
"against the claims of myself, my heirs, … any person or persons whatsoever"	A **limited warranty** of title: Parish guarantees no one can successfully contest Matthews's ownership.
Court proof & recordation	Under 1801 NC law, two witnesses plus a court-room acknowledgement were required to **register** the deed and give **public notice**.

273

Know all men by these presents that I James Robeson of Guilford County for & in consideration of the Sum of 465 Silver Dollars to me in hand paid by Isaac Lane of Randolph County at & before the Sealing & Delivery of these presents the Receipt whereof is hereby acknowledged have Bargained & Sold & by these presents Doath Grant Bargain & Sell unto the s^d^ Isaac Lane three Negros (to wit) one woman by the Name of Anecia aged 26 one Boy Named Willis aged three years one Girl Named Silva aged seven Months To Have & to Hold the s^d^ Negroes Slaves & their Increase by these presents Bargained & Sold & Granted unto the only Proper use & Behoof of the s^d^ Isaac Lane his Heirs Exec^rs^ & Adm^rs^ & assigns forever & the s^d^ James Robeson for my Self my heirs Exe^r^ & Adm^r^ & assigns forever I the s^d^ James Robeson for my Self my Heirs Exe^r^ & Adm^r^ all & Singular the s^d^ Slaves unto the s^d^ Isaac Lane his Heirs & assigns against me the s^d^ James Robeson my Heirs & assigns against all & every other person & persons Whatsoever Will Warrant & forever defend by these presents In Witness whereof I the s^d^ James Robeson have hereunto Set my hand & Seal the 1st Day of January A^D^ 1801

State of N^o^ Carolina }
Randolph County } August Term 1801

The Execution of the above Bill of Sale was duly proved in open Court by John Brower & ordered to be Registered

Copy Test — Harper Clk

542

This Indenture Made the 27th Day of November in the year 1801 Between David Moss of the County of Randolph State of N^o^ Carolina of the one part & Robert Holaday of the County of Orange & State afs^d^ of the other part Witnesseth that the s^d^ David Moss for and in consideration of the Sum of 500 Dollars to him in hand paid the Receipt whereof is hereby acknowledged hath Granted Bargained & Sold & by these presents Doath Grant Bargain & Sell Alien & Confirm unto the s^d^ Robert Holaday his Heirs & assigns a Certain piece or parcel of Land lying in s^d^ County of Randolph on Stone Waters Beg^g^ at a pine & Running South 40 Ch^s^ to a pine, then East 24 Ch^s^ to a pine, then N° 40 Ch^s^ to a pine, then West 92 Ch^s^ to a Stake, then N° 20 Ch^s^ to a Black Oak, in the original line Corner of the 30 acre tract then S^o^ 75 W^t^ 25 Ch^s^ to a White Oak, then S^o^ 47 E^t^ 12 Ch^s^ to a Black Oak, then to the Beginning Cont^g^ 130 Acres be the Same More or less Together with all Mines Minerals Woods Waters Ways Commodities Advantages & appurtenances Whatsoever Belonging or in any wise appertaining & also the Reversion & Reversions Remainder & Remainders Rents & Services of the s^d^ Premises & of every part thereof & all the Estate Right title Interest Claim & Demand Whatsoever of him the s^d^ David Moss of in & to the s^d^ piece or parcel of Land & premises & every part thereof To Have & To Hold the s^d^ piece or parcel of Land with the appurtenances unto the s^d^ Robert Holaday his Heirs & assigns to the only Proper use & Behoof of him the s^d^ Robert Holaday his Heirs & assigns forever & he the s^d^ David Moss for himself & his Heirs & against all and Every other person or persons Whatsoever unto the s^d^ Robert Holaday his Heirs & assigns Shall Warrant & forever Defend by these presents In Witness whereof the s^d^ David Moss hath hereunto Set his hand & affixed his Seal the Day & year above Written —

State of N^o^ Carolina }
Randolph County } August Term 1801

The Execution of the above Deed of Conveyance is duly Proved in open Court by Samuel Millikan & ordered to be Registered

Copy Test — Harper Clk

Source location	Randolph County (NC)
Book / page	8 / 273
Date	January 1, 1804
Consideration	465 silver dollars
Type	Bill of Sale
Grantor	James Roberson
Grantee	Isaac Lane
Abstract	Three Negroes: woman named Aneca[unclear], 26; boy named Willis, 3; and girl named Selve, 7 months. Grantor is of Guilford County

Instrument A Bill of Sale of Three Slaves

(James Adkinson → Jesse Lowe; 1 Jan 1801; proved Aug 1801)

1. Diplomatic Transcription

Know all men by these presents that I, **James Adkinson** of Guilford County, for and in consideration of the sum of **465 dollars** to me in hand paid by **Jesse Lowe** of Randolph County at and before the delivery & delivery of these presents the receipt whereof I do hereby acknowledge,

have bargained & sold & by these presents do grant bargain & sell & deliver unto the said Jesse Lowe **three negroes, to wit,** one woman by the name of **Annica**, aged 26; one boy named **Willie**, aged three years; one girl named **Louisa**, aged three months; **to have & to hold** the said negroes slaves & their increase **unto the said Jesse Lowe his heirs & assigns for ever**, and I do hereby warrant and defend the right & title of the said slaves to him, the said Jesse Lowe, for myself, my heirs, executors & administrators & appoint forever the said Jesse Lowe his heirs & assigns against me the said James Adkinson my heirs & assigns against all person & persons whatsoever.

In witness whereof I have hereunto set my hand & affixed my seal this **1s□ day of January A.D. 1801**.

(Seal) James Adkinson
Sealed and delivered
in the presence of Benjamin Hoppitt

State of North Carolina, Randolph County
Court of Pleas & Quarter Sessions, August Term 1801
The execution of the above bill of sale was duly proved in open court by John Brown & ordered to be registered.
Copy Test A. Harper, Clk.

2. Plain-English Rendering

Sale of Three Enslaved Persons
I, **James Adkinson**, for **$465 paid by Jesse Lowe**, hereby sell and deliver to him (and to his heirs and assigns forever) these three enslaved people:

1. **Annica**, a woman about age 26

2. **Willie**, a boy about age 3

3. **Louisa**, a girl about age 3 months
   I warrant that I lawfully own them and that no one else has any claim.

Executed **1 January 1801**. A Randolph County court (Aug 1801) heard witness John Brown and ordered this bill of sale recorded.

3. Clause-by-Clause Notes

Phrase	**Purpose & Effect**
"consideration … 465 dollars"	Documents the exact **purchase price**, settled in hand, preventing later dispute.
"bargained & sold … do grant bargain & sell & deliver"	Series of **granting words** effecting absolute transfer of ownership.
Naming of each slave + age	Identifies each person unambiguously by name and approximate age.
"to have & to hold … for ever"	Conveys permanent, inheritable ownership.
"warrant and defend the right & title … against all persons whatsoever"	A **limited warranty** ensuring Jesse Lowe's ownership cannot be overturned by any lawful claim.
Witness & court proof	One witnessing oath plus **open-court acknowledgment** were required in 1801 NC to **register** a slave sale, giving public notice and legal effect.

Know all Men by these presents that I Simeon Gunn of Randolph County & State of N. Carolina and in consideration of one hundred & fifty pounds to me in hand paid by Josh Bagley of Chatham County & State afs.d at or before the Sealing & Delivering of these presents the Receipt whereof is hereby acknowledged have Bargained & Sold & by these presents Doth Grant Bargain & Sell unto the s.d Josh Bagley one Negro Woman Slave by the Name of Jane & one Boy Child by the Name of Hardy To have & to hold the s.d Slaves by these presents have Bargained Sold & Granted unto the Only proper use & behoof of the said Josh Bagley his Heirs Exec.s Adm.s & Assigns forever & I the s.d Simeon Gunn for my Self my Heirs Exec.s Adm.s all & Singular the s.d Slaves unto the s.d Josh Bagley his Heirs & Assigns against me the s.d Simeon Gunn my Heirs & Assigns & against all & every Other person or persons Whatsoever Will Warrant & forever Defend by these presents In Witness Whereof I the said Simeon Gunn have hereunto Set my hand & Seal this 24 Day of February 1797

State of North Carolina }
Randolph County } May Term 1797
The Execution of the above Bill of Sale was duly Acknowledged in open Court by Simeon Gunn & ordered to be Registered
A true Copy Test J Harper Clk

Know all men by these presents that I Walter Wisley of Orange County & State of N. Carolina have Bargained Sold & Delivered & by these presents do Bargain Sell & Deliver unto Benjamin Means of Randolph County and Negro Boy Named Prime aged about 25 years for the Consideration of Two Hundred & Eighty Dollars Which s.d Negro Boy I do hereby Warrant from all Lawfull Claims & Demands Whatsoever To be Healthy & clear of any unseen impediment to my knowledge unto the Said Benjamin Means & his Heirs & Assigns forever In Witness Whereof I have hereunto Set my hand and Seal this 9th Day of February 1797

State of North Carolina }
Randolph County } May Term 1797
the Execution of the within Bill of Sale was duly proved in open Court by James Elder & ordered to be Registered
Copy Test J Harper Clk

Source location	Randolph County (NC)
Book / page	7 / 170
Date	February 25, 1797
Consideration	£150
Type	Bill of Sale
Grantor	Simeon Geron
Grantee	Joab Bagley
Abstract	Negro woman slave named Joan and boy child named Hardy. Grantee is indexed as Jacob Bagley

No. 249 Bill of Sale of Three Enslaved Persons

(Simon Gunn → Isaac Wagley; 21 Feb 1797; proved May 1797)

1. Diplomatic Transcription

249
Know all men by these presents that I, **Simon Gunn** of the county of Randolph and state of North Carolina, for and in consideration of **one hundred & fifty pounds** to me in hand paid by **Isaac Wagley** of Randolph County & state aforesaid (the receipt whereof I do hereby acknowledge),
have bargained & sold & by these presents do grant, bargain & sell & alien unto the said **Isaac Wagley**, his heirs & assigns forever, **one negro woman slave by the name of Annicia, aged 26 years; one boy named Willie, aged three years; one girl named Louisa, aged three months; and the future increase of the said woman**, to have and to hold the said negroes and their increase unto the said Isaac Wagley, his heirs & assigns forever;
and I the said Simon Gunn, for myself, my heirs, executors & administrators, **do covenant to warrant & forever defend** the title of the said slaves to the said Isaac Wagley, his heirs & assigns, **against me the said Simon Gunn, my heirs & assigns, and against all & every other person or persons whatsoever**.

In witness whereof I have hereunto set my hand & seal this **21st day of February A.D. 1797**.

(Seal) Simon Gunn
Sealed & delivered in presence of
Samuel Giles

State of North Carolina, Randolph County
Court of Pleas & Quarter Sessions, May Term 1797
The execution of the above bill of sale was duly proved in open court by Samuel Giles & ordered to be registered.
copy test Harper Clk

---

2. Modern-English Rendering

Sale of a Woman and Two Children (Feb 21 1797)
I, **Simon Gunn** of Randolph County, NC, for **£150** paid by **Isaac Wagley**, hereby sell to him (and to his heirs and assigns forever):

- **Annicia**, a woman slave about age 26
- **Willie**, a boy slave about age 3
- **Louisa**, a girl slave about age 3 months
  and **all future children** born to Annicia.
  I guarantee to Isaac Wagley (and his heirs/assigns) good title free of any

claims by me, my heirs, or anyone else.

Signed 21 February 1797; in May 1797 the county court heard witness Samuel Giles and ordered the deed recorded.

---

3. Clause-by-Clause Notes

Phrase	**Function**
"consideration of one hundred & fifty pounds"	Fixes the **sale price** (£150), paid in hand.
"have bargained & sold & by these presents do grant … alien"	Canonical **granting/bargain-and-sale language** effecting an immediate transfer of the enslaved persons.
"one negro woman slave …; one boy …; one girl …; and the future increase"	Identifies each person by **name and age**, plus any **future offspring** (ensuring the buyer acquires the entire matrilineal line).
"to have and to hold … forever"	Conveys a **permanent, inheritable** ownership interest.
"do covenant to warrant & forever defend … against all & every other person"	A **general warranty**: Gunn promises to **defend** Wagley's title against any lawful claim, whether by Gunn himself or anyone else.
Witness & court proof	Under 1797 law, one eyewitness oath (Samuel Giles) plus an **open-court acknowledgment** were required to **register** the sale, giving public notice and legal effect.

No. 250 Bill of Sale of One Enslaved Boy

(Waller Wagley → Benjamin Gunn; 17 Feb 1797; proved May 1797)

1. Diplomatic Transcription

250
Know all men by these presents that I, **Waller Wagley** of Randolph county & State of North Carolina, **have bargained & sold & delivered & by these presents do bargain & sell & deliver** unto **Benjamin Gunn** of Randolph county, **one negro boy named Bono, aged about twenty-five years**, for the consideration of **two hundred & eighty dollars** (receipt whereof is hereby acknowledged);
and I the said Waller Wagley, for myself, my heirs & assigns, **do hereby warrant from all lawful claims & demands whatsoever, to be healthy & clear of body & a slave of my own free & clear of all encumbrance to my knowledge**, unto the said Benjamin Gunn, his heirs & assigns forever;

and I the said Waller Wagley, for myself, my heirs & assigns, **against all & every other person or persons whatsoever, will warrant & forever defend by these presents**.
In witness whereof the said Waller Wagley hath hereunto set my hand & seal this **17□^{h} day of February 1797**.

(Seal) Waller Wagley
Sealed & delivered
in presence of
James Giles

State of North Carolina, Randolph County
Court of Pleas & Quarter Sessions, May Term 1797
The execution of the within bill of sale was duly proved in open court by James Giles & ordered to be registered.
copy test Harper Clk

---

2. Modern-English Rendering

Sale of a 25-Year-Old Boy (Feb 17 1797)
I, **Waller Wagley** of Randolph County, NC, for **$280** paid by **Benjamin Gunn**, hereby sell to him (and to his heirs and assigns forever) **Bono**, a **25-year-old boy slave**.
I warrant that Bono is healthy, that I lawfully own him free of any liens or claims to my knowledge, and I will defend Benjamin Gunn's title against any and all claims.

Signed 17 February 1797; at the May 1797 court the signature was proved by James Giles, and the deed was recorded.

---

3. Clause-by-Clause Notes

Phrase	**Function**
"consideration of two hundred & eighty dollars"	Fixes the **sale price** ($280), paid in hand.
"have bargained & sold & deliver … do bargain & sell & deliver"	Standard **bargain-and-sale language** ensuring clear transfer.
"one negro boy named Bono, aged about twenty-five years"	Identifies the enslaved individual by **name and age**.
"warrant from all lawful claims & demands whatsoever"	A **limited warranty**: Wagley guarantees no one else has a lawful claim to Bono.
"healthy & clear of body & a slave of my own free & clear of all encumbrance"	Affirms the

boy's **sound health** and the grantor's **unencumbered ownership**. |
| "will warrant & forever defend … against all & every other person" | A **general warranty** promising legal defense of the buyer's title. |
| **Witness & court proof** | One witness (James Giles) plus an open-court acknowledgment were required for **registration**, making the sale a matter of public record. |

Why These Matter

Together, Nos. 249 and 250 show:

- **How people were described** (by name, age, offspring) in 1790s slave-sale deeds.
- **The role of "consideration"** (money paid in hand) in sealing each transfer.
- **The use of both limited and general warranty language** to protect buyers' titles to human chattel.
- **The formalities of early North Carolina law**—a witnessing oath plus open-court acknowledgment—to ensure that every sale, of land or of persons, was duly recorded and publicly known.

This Indenture Made this Twenty Seventh day of December one thousand Seven Hundred & Ninety Seven Between Solomon Roach of the County of Randolph & State of North Carolina of the one part & his three Children of the other part to wit Rebecca Roach Peyton Roach & Prisilla Roach Witnesseth That the Sd. Solomon Roach for & in the Consideration of the Sum of Five Pounds Each to wit five pounds from Rebecca Roach five Pounds from Peyton Roach & five pounds from Prisilla Roach Cash in hand paid the Receipt whereof the Said Solomon Roach doath hereby Acknowledge he the Sd. Solomon Roach hath Given Granted Bargained & Sold & by these Presents doath Give Grant Bargain & Sell unto the Sd. Children the following Negroes to wit Grace a Child of Rose about Six years old to my Daughter Rebecca to her & her Heirs forever Reserving the Life of My Wife Hannah Roach in the Sd. Negro Girl Grace Stafford to Peyton Roach a son of Rose about the Age of three years old Reserving the Life of my Wife in him also to him & his Heirs forever & likewise Patt a Daughter of Rose to Prisilla about four years of Age to her & her Heirs forever Reserving the Life of my Wife Hannah Roach in her also the whole Each of them To Have & to Hold the Sd. Negro Children as above Mentioned to wit Grace to Rebecca Roach Stafford to Peyton Roach & Patt to Prisilla Roach Reserving the Life of Hannah Roach to them their Heirs & Assigns to the only Proper use & Behoof of the Sd. Rebecca Roach Peyton Roach & Prisilla Roach to them their Heirs & Assigns forever & the Sd. Solomon Roach doath for himself & his Heirs Exrs. Admrs. Covenant & agree to & with the Sd. Rebecca Roach with Peyton Roach & with Prisilla Roach their Heirs & Assigns by these Presents that he the Sd. Solomon Roach & his Heirs Exrs. Admrs. & Assigns will forever Warrant & defend the Right & Title of the Sd. Negroes Grace Stafford & Patt hereby Bargained & Sold to the Sd. Rebecca Roach Peyton Roach & Prisilla Roach & to their Heirs & Assigns forever against the Claim of any other Person or persons Whatever Lawfully Claiming any Right or Title in & to the Sd. Negroes Grace Stafford & Patt In Witness Whereof the Sd. Solomon Roach hath hereunto Set his Name & Affixed his Seal the Day & year above Written

State of No. Carolina }
Randolph County } May Term 1798
The Execution of the above Bill of Sale from Solomon Roach to his Three Children Viz. Rebecca Roach Peyton Roach & Prisilla Roach was [illegible] Proven in open Court by [illegible] & ordered to be Registered

Source location	Randolph County (NC)
Book / page	7 / 329
Date	December 27, 1797
Consideration	-
Type	Deed Gift
Grantor	Solomon Poarch
Grantee	Rebecca, Payton, and Prissilla Poarch
Abstract	To Rebecca: Grace, about 6, a child of Rose. To Payton: Stafford Stafford, 3, a son of Rose. To Prissilla: Patt, about 4, a daughter of Rose. The slaves are reserved to grantor's wife Hannah during her lifetime.

1. Diplomatic Transcription

No. 253

This Indenture made the Twenty seventh day of November one thousand seven hundred & ninety seven

Between Richard Beach of the County of Randolph & State of North Carolina of

the one part,
and Thomas Beach of the County & State aforesaid of the other part.
Witnesseth that the said **Richard Beach**, for and in consideration of the **sum of five pounds current money** to him in hand paid by **the said Thomas Beach**, the receipt whereof he doth hereby acknowledge,
hath granted, bargained, sold and delivered, and by these presents doth **grant, bargain, sell and convey** unto the said **Thomas Beach**, his heirs and assigns forever, **the following negro slaves**, to wit:

1. **Grace Stafford**, a little girl slave about **nineteen years** of age;

2. **Grace Stafford Jr.**, a boy slave of about **ten years** of age;

3. **Betty**, a daughter slave of about **four years** of age;
   all of whom are now in the possession of **Hannah Beach**, wife of the said Richard Beach, to have and to hold the said slaves — and the increase of the said Grace Stafford (the mother) — **unto the said Thomas Beach**, his heirs and assigns forever.
   And the said **Richard Beach** for himself, his heirs, executors and administrators, **covenants** with the said Thomas Beach, his heirs and assigns, that he is **lawfully seized** in fee simple of the premises; has **good right** to convey the same; that the premises are **free from all incumbrances**; and that he will **warrant and forever defend** the title against all persons lawfully claiming by, through or under him.
   In witness whereof the said **Richard Beach** hath hereunto set his hand and affixed his seal the day and year above written.

(Seal) Richard Beach
Sealed & delivered in presence of
John Thames
John McCoy

State of North Carolina, Randolph County
Court of Pleas & Quarter Sessions, May Term 1798
The execution of the above indenture was duly proved in open court by John Thames & ordered to be registered.
Copy Test Harper, Clk.

---

2. Modern-English Translation

Sale of Three Enslaved Children (Nov 27, 1797)
I, **Richard Beach** of Randolph County, for **£5 paid by Thomas Beach**, hereby sell to him (and to his heirs and assigns forever) the following enslaved persons, now held by my wife Hannah Beach:

1. **Grace Stafford**, a girl about 19 years old

2. **Grace Stafford Jr.**, a boy about 10 years old

3. **Betty**, a girl about 4 years old
   I warrant that I legally own them outright; that there are no liens or claims on them; and I will defend Thomas Beach's title against anyone.

Signed 27 Nov 1797; and in May 1798 the county court proved the signature (witness John Thames) and ordered the deed recorded.

---

3. Clause-by-Clause Notes

Original Phrase	**Function**
—	—
"for and in consideration of the sum of five pounds"	Records the exact price (£5) paid, "in hand," to prevent dispute.
"hath granted, bargained, sold and delivered … grant, bargain, sell and convey"	A full set of **legal verbs** effecting an absolute transfer of ownership.
Naming each slave + age	Identifies the three enslaved children by name and approximate age, plus "increase of the said Grace" (i.e. any future children she bears).
"to have and to hold … forever"	Conveys a **fee-simple** estate in the persons, i.e. perpetual, inheritable ownership.
General warranty covenant: • "lawfully seized" • "good right to convey" • "free from all incumbrances" • "warrant and forever defend"	Guarantees to the buyer (Thomas Beach) that the grantor (Richard Beach) truly owns the human property outright, that nothing else claims it, and that he will defend that title forever.
Witnesses + court proof	Under 1797 NC law, one witness oath plus **open-court acknowledgment** were **mandatory** to record a slave sale, putting the world on notice and giving the deed legal force.

Why It Matters

- **Price**: £5 for three children in 1797 reflects depressed market conditions just after the Revolution.

- **Family break-up**: Mother Grace's "increase" is explicitly conveyed, but no mention of father or wider kin.

- **Survivor estate**: The deed ensures Hannah Beach will no longer have any claim to her own children.

- **Formalities**: Witness and court steps made the transfer a matter of public record, protecting Thomas Beach's title at the clerk's office in Asheboro for generations to come.

This Indenture Made this 4th Day of January in the year of our Lord 1799 Between Abraham Williams of the County of Green & State of Tenesee of the one part and Samuel Nelson of the County of Randolph & State of No Carolina of the other part Witnesseth that the Sd Abraham Williams for & in consideration of the Sum of one Hundred pounds Current Money to him in hand paid by the Sd Samuel Nelson the Receipt whereof he doth hereby Acknowledge hath Granted Bargained & Sold Aliened & Confirmed & by these presents Doth Grant bargain & Sell Alien & Confirm unto the Sd Samuel Nelson his Heirs & Assigns all that tract or parcel of Land Lying in Sd County & State afsd on the Watters of Mill Stoney Creek Being the West End or part of a Tract of three Hundred Acres Begining at a post Oak Robert Barkers Corner Running North on Robert Barkers line 64 po. to a post Oak Sd Barkers Corner thence West 60 po. to a Blackjack by the Cross Creek Road thence So 25 E. along Sd Road 60 po. to a post Oak then So 8 Do Et along Sd Road 52 po. to a Black Jack then So 25 Et 146 po. to a Blackjack Bounded by Robert Rains Et 85 ½ po. to a Black Jack a Corner Between Sd Nelson & Hart thence No 176 po to a Spanish Oak in Robert Barkers line thence West on Sd Barkers line to the place of Begining Containing one Hundred & fifty Acres Together With all mines Minerals Woods Watters Ways Commodities Advantages & Appurtenances Whatsoever to the Sd Message Belonging or in anywise Appertaining & Also the Reversion & Reversions Remainder & Remainders Rents & Services What soever of the Sd Premises & Every part thereof To Have & To Hold the Sd Tract or parcel of Land with the Appurtenances unto the Sd Samuel Nelson his Heirs & Assigns to the only proper use & Behoof of him the Sd Samuel Nelson his Heirs & Assigns forever & he the Sd Abraham Williams for himself & his Heirs & Against All & Every other person or persons Whatsoever unto the Sd Samuel Nelson his Heirs & Assigns Shall & will Warrant & forever Defend by these presents In Witness Whereof the Sd Abraham Williams hath hereunto Set his hand & affixed his Seal the Day & year first above Written

State of No Carolina }
Randolph County } February Term 1799 The Execution of the above Deed of Conveyance was duly proved in Open Court by John Lane & Ordered to be Registered Copy Test Harper

---

Know all Men by these presents that we William Bell & Thomas Carson Executors of the Estate of Richard Tyson Decd. in order to Satisfy Sundry Judgements & Execution against Sd Estate have a Negro Girl Named Sal ... up at publick Vendue in the Town of Lexington on Saturday the 2d of February 1799 At Which Sale Abraham Gossett of the County of Randolph & State of No Carolina Became the Last & Highest Bidder in pursuance of Which we Do hereby Warrant & Defend the Sd Negro Girl to the Sd Abraham Gossett his Heirs & Assigns Against All Lawfull Claims or Demands Whatever Witness our Hands & Seals this 2d Day of February 1799

State of No Carolina }
Randolph County } Feby Term 1799 The Execution of the above ~~Deed of Conveyance~~ Bill of Sale Was duly proved in Open Court By Daniel Clawson & Ordered To be Registered Copy Test Harper Clk

---

Know all men by these presents that I Jesse Teetal of No Carolina & Randolph County for and in Consideration of the Sum of Two Hundred & Ten Dollars to me in hand paid by Simeon Gunn of the County & State afsd the Receipt Whereof is Hereby Acknowledged have Bargained & Sold & by these presents doth Bargain Sell & Deliver unto the Sd Simeon Gunn one Negro Girl Slave Named Nancy Eleven years of Age Clear of all Bodily Infirmities Which Sd Negro I Do Hereby Warrant & forever Defend from any Claim or Claims Whatever from my Self my Heirs & Assigns forever unto the Sd Simeon Gunn his Heirs & Assigns forever In Witness Whereof I have hereunto Set my Hand & Seal this 27th Day of October 1797

State of North Carolina } February Term 1799 — The Execution of the above Bill of Sale
Randolph County } Was duly proved in Open Court by Isaac Lane & ordered to be Registered Copy Test Harper Clk

Source location	Randolph County (NC)
Book / page	8 / 49
Date	February 2, 1799
Consideration	unspecified
Type	Bill of Sale
Grantor	William Bell, Thomas Carson
Grantee	Abraham Gossett
Abstract	Negro girl from estate of Richard Lyons, sold publicly in Lexington

Indenture A

Date: 8 January 1799
Parties:

- **Grantor:** Abraham Williams (Randolph Co., NC)

- **Grantee:** Samuel Nelson (Randolph Co., NC)

Diplomatic Transcription

This Indenture made the 8th day of January in the year of our Lord 1799

Between Abraham Williams of the County of **Randolph** & State of North Carolina of the one part

and Samuel Nelson of the County & State aforesaid of the other part.

Witnesseth that the said Abraham Williams, for and in consideration of the sum of **one hundred pounds current money**, to him in hand paid by the said Samuel Nelson (the receipt whereof he doth hereby acknowledge),

Hath granted, bargained & sold, aliened & confirmed, and by these presents doth **grant, bargain, sell, alien & confirm** unto the said Samuel Nelson, his heirs & assigns, **all that tract or parcel of land**, lying in the County & State aforesaid, on the Waters of **Stock–ton Creek**, being the West End or part of a Tract of **three thousand acres**, running as follows, to wit:

Beginning at a post oak **Robert Bashoor's** corner; running North on Robert Bashoor's line 64 poles to a post oak, S 5° W 28 p; to a black jack, thence N 60° W 72 p; to a blackjack & remaining on said Bashoor's line 25 p; along said line W 6 ¼° S 42 p; to a black jack, thence N 25° E 146 p; to a blackjack & bounded by Robert Bashoor & 9 yse½ p to a black jack & corner between said Nelson & said *William McElroy*'s lot; thence N 76 ¼° W 160 p to a Spanish oak in Robert Bashoor's line; thence West on Bashoor's line to the place of beginning, containing **one hundred & fifty acres**, together with **all mines, minerals, woods, waters, ways, commodious advantages & appurtenances whatsoever** to the said tract of land belonging, or in anywise appertaining, and **the reversion & reversions, remainder & remainders, rents & services** of the same.

To have and to hold the said parcel of land, with the appurtenances, unto the said Samuel Nelson, his heirs & assigns, to the only proper use & behoof of the said Samuel Nelson, in fee simple, and he, the said Abraham Williams, for himself, his heirs & assigns, **doth covenant & agree** to and with the said Samuel Nelson, his heirs & assigns, that the said tract of land is and shall be **warranted & forever defend** by these presents.

In witness whereof the said Abraham Williams hath hereunto set his hand and affixed his seal the day & year first above written.

(Seal) Abraham Williams

Sealed & delivered
in presence of
John McNeese
David Ballard

State of North Carolina, Randolph County—**February Term 1799**—
The execution of the above Deed of Conveyance was duly proved in open court by David Ballard & ordered to be Registered.
Copy Test: Harper Clk.

Modern-English Translation

Land Sale (8 Jan 1799)
I, **Abraham Williams** of Randolph County, NC, for **£100 current money** paid by **Samuel Nelson**, sell and convey to him (and to his heirs and assigns forever) **150 acres** on Stockton Creek (described by bounding lines above), together with every right, benefit, watercourse, mineral, way, "reversion," and service. I warrant that I own it outright in fee simple, that it is free of all encumbrances, and will defend Nelson's title forever.

Signed & sealed 8 Jan 1799; proved and recorded at February Term 1799.

Clause-by-Clause Notes

Phrase	**Comment**
"for … one hundred pounds current money"	Exact purchase price (§ consideration).
"grant, bargain, sell, alien & confirm"	Full suite of conveyancing verbs to transfer fee-simple title.
"tract or parcel of land … containing one hundred & fifty acres"	Precise acreage; "West End" of larger 3,000 acre survey.
Metes & Bounds	Orientation by compass bearings and distances (poles) tied to neighbor Robert Bashoor's line.
"all mines, minerals, woods, waters, ways, commodious advantages & appurtenances"	Conveys every ancillary right—timber, water-power, easements, etc.
"reversion & reversions, remainder & remainders, rents & services"	Technical terms preserving any future interests or rents.
General warranty covenant	Grantor promises absolute title in fee simple, free from encumbrance, with perpetual defense.
Witnesses + court proof	Two subscribing witnesses + open-court acknowledgment required under 1799 NC law for land deeds.

Indenture B

Date: February Term 1801
Parties:

- **Grantors:** William Bell & Thomas Carson, Executors of Christian Seigler, dec'd
- **Grantee:** Abraham Seigler

Diplomatic Transcription

Know all men by these presents that we William Bell & Thomas Carson, Executors of the Estate of Christian Seigler, late of Randolph County, dec'd, **in order to satisfy a Judgment & Execution against the said Estate,**
Have a negro girl named **Betty**, about fourteen years old, **to sell** at public vendue in the town of **Asheboro** on the 2^d day of February 1801;
At which vendue the said negro girl was struck off to **Abraham Seigler**, the last and highest bidder, in presence of us (the undersigned).
Whereupon we do hereby **warrant & defend** the title of the said negro girl to the said Abraham Seigler, his heirs & assigns, against all lawful claims or demands whatsoever.
Witness our hands & seals this 2^d day of February 1801.

(Seal) William Bell (Seal) Thomas Carson
State of North Carolina, Randolph County—**February Term 1801**—
The execution of the above Bill of Sale was duly proved in open court by Samuel Millikan & ordered to be Registered.
Copy Test: Harper Clk.

Modern-English Translation

Sale by Executors (Feb 1801)
We, **William Bell** and **Thomas Carson**, executors of the estate of **Christian Seigler** (deceased), to satisfy a judgment on that estate, **sell at public auction** a **14-year-old enslaved girl "Betty"**. On 2 Feb 1801 in Asheboro she was knocked down to **Abraham Seigler** for the highest bid. We warrant that she belongs to the estate and will defend his title against all claims.

Witnessed 2 Feb 1801; proved and recorded in open court the same term.

Clause-by-Clause Notes

Phrase	Comment
"in order to satisfy a Judgment & Execution"	Shows this is a **forced sale** by estate executors.
"public vendue … struck off to"	Auction method; "struck off" = knocked down to highest bidder.
"last and highest bidder"	Confirms Abraham Seigler paid the final bid.
General warranty covenant	Executors guarantee the estate's title, despite compelled sale.
Witness & court proof	Executors' oath + court docketing required for validity.

Why This Page Matters

- **Indenture A** is a **straightforward purchase** of frontier acreage for £100—an example of settlement-era land transfers.
- **Indenture B** is a **judicial sale** of a 14-year-old girl "Betty," illustrating how enslaved people were treated as chattel collateral in North Carolina courts.
- In both deeds you see the **same formalities**: full conveyancing language, metes & bounds (land), or auction detail (slave), plus witness signatures and county-court acknowledgment to make each record permanent.

Together, these two instruments lay bare the intertwined practices of land speculation and human bondage in Randolph County at the turn of the 19th century.

(378) To All people whom these presents shall come I William Alred do send Greeting Know ye that I William Alred of the County of Randolph & State of No Carolina for & in consideration of the Love & good will & affection which I have & do bear towards my son William Alred of the Sd County of Randolph have given & granted & by these presents do freely give & grant unto the Sd William Alred his heirs & assigns forever all & singular that tract or parcel of Land Situate in the Sd County of Randolph the place whereon he now dwells on the waters of Deep River Beginning at a willow oak on the River Bank the original corner & Runing North along the original line 38 poles to a black Jack thence N. 34 E. 41 poles to a small persimon thence S. 67 E. 2 poles to a white oak stump thence N. 20 E. 36 poles to a high white oak stump thence S. 25 E. 9 poles to a stake thence S. 65 E. 32 poles to a Black oak thence S. 25 W. 20 poles to a Hickory thence S. 61 E. 48 poles to the creek the same course nearly continued down the creek to the old line thence South along Sd line crossing Deep River 117 poles to a black oak thence West 118 poles to a black oak near the River thence to the Beginning Containing in the whole one hundred & thirty four acres it being part of two tracts which the Sd William Alred entered out of the office the one bearing date Decr the 11th 1762 the other September the 9th 1779 be it more or be it less To have & to hold said premises & every part thereof to him his heirs & assigns forever as his other proper goods & chattles freely by them & him possessed absolutely without any manner of condition as witness my hand & seal this 18th day of August in the year 1800

State of No Carolina }
Randolph County } August Term 1800

The Execution of the within deed of conveyance was duly acknowledged in open Court & ordered to be registered

Test
Copy Test H Harper Clk

382

Know all men by these presents that I Isaac Lane High Sheriff of the County of Randolph & State of No Carolina by virtue of a writ to me directed returnable to the County Court of Caswell July Term Next against Nathaniel Cunningham Reference thereto being made will more fully appear have seized on a certain Female Negro by the Name of Letty a slave late the property of Sd Nathaniel Cunningham & after having exposed Sd Negro at public sale agreeable to Law the Sd Negro was cried off to John Hunt he being the highest Bidder for 291 Dollars & a half which Sd Negro I do hereby grant bargain & sell & by virtue of my office do by these presents grant bargain sell & deliver Sd Negro Slave to John Hunt his heirs & assigns forever & I do & will warrant & defend forever defend by these presents against all & every person whatever the Sd Negro Girl named Letty to the Sd John Hunt his heirs & assigns forever In witness whereof I have hereunto set my hand & affixed my seal this 16th day of June in the year 1800

State of No Carolina }
Randolph County } August Term 1800

The Execution of the above bill of sale was duly acknowledged in open Court by Isaac Lane Shff & and ordered to be registered

Test
Copy Test H Harper Clk

383

Know all men by these presents that we Harris Kimbal & [illegible] Kimbal of the County of Randolph & State of No Carolina for & in consideration of the sum of Sixty five pounds to us in hand paid by John Atherton of the County & State afsd the receipt whereof we do hereby acknowledge have Remised Released & forever Quit Claimed & do by these presents Remise Release & forever Quit Claim unto John Atherton his heirs & assigns forever all our right [illegible] of that tract or parcel of Land late of the Estate of William [illegible] deceased lying & being in the County aforesd Bounded as follows (viz) Beginning at Stones corner stake on the West Side of the [illegible] thence Runing [illegible] 40 poles to a stake then West 84 poles to a stake in the old line then South

Source location	Randolph County (NC)
Book / page	8 / 178
Date	June 6, 1800
Consideration	$291.50
Type	Bill of Sale
Grantor	Isaac Lane, Sheriff
Grantee	John Fruit

[certificate, closing a prior indenture]

…and assigns forever.

And the said party of the first part, for the consideration aforesaid, doth hereby covenant and agree to warrant and defend the premises aforesaid to the said party of the second part, his executors, administrators & assigns, against the claims and demands of all persons whatsoever; and doth further covenant, that he is seized of the premises in fee simple and hath power to make and convey such an estate by this Indenture; and hath done the same by these presents.

In witness whereof, the said party of the first part hath hereunto set his hand and seal on the day and year above written.

Signed, sealed and delivered
in presence of
Benj'n Huffstetler
Humfrey Brown (seal)

North Carolina }
Randolph County } Court of Pleas & Quarter Sessions, February Term 1805
The due execution of the within deed is duly acknowledged by the grantor in open court, and a State and County tax of three dollars paid. Let said deed together with this certificate be registered.

(Registered Feb'y 16th 1805.)

J. H. Brown, Clk.

382

Gift from Alexander Gazy to his son Julius A. Gazy

Know all men by these presents, that I
Alexander Gazy **of the County of Randolph and State of North Carolina, for and in consideration of the regard and affection which I have toward my son Julius A. Gazy, and for his advancement, and also for and in consideration of the sum of five dollars to me in hand paid by the said Julius A. Gazy, the receipt whereof I do hereby acknowledge, have given, granted, devised, bargained and sold unto the said Julius A. Gazy three negro men, slaves, viz.:**

- **Gus, aged twenty-five years;**
- **Wiley, aged twenty years;**
- **Dan Brown, aged eighteen years;**

all of which slaves are sound and healthy; and I do hereby warrant and defend the right and title of said slaves to him the said Julius A. Gazy, free from the claim or claims of any person or persons whatsoever.

In witness whereof, I have hereunto set my hand and affixed my seal this thirtieth day of December, A.D. 1859.

Signed Alexander Gazy (seal)
Attest Alfred C. Foster

State of North Carolina }
Randolph County } May Term 1865
The execution of the foregoing deed of gift is proved in open court by the oath of A. C. Foster, subscribing witness to the same. Let said deed together with this

certificate be registered.

(Registered Feb'y 16[] h 1865.)

J. H. Brown, Clk.

383

Bill of Sale from Jesse Lane

Know all men by these presents, that I
Jesse Lane **of the County of Randolph and State of North Carolina, for and in consideration of the sum of—dollars to me in hand paid by—of—County & State aforesaid, the receipt whereof I do hereby acknowledge, have bargained and sold and by these presents do bargain and sell unto the said—his heirs and assigns forever one negro girl slave named—aged about—years, to have and to hold the said slave unto the said—his heirs & assigns forever, and I do hereby warrant and defend the right and title of the said slave to him the said—his heirs and assigns against the claim or claims of all persons whatsoever.**

In witness whereof, I have hereunto set my hand and affixed my seal this—day of—A.D. 18—.

Signed Jesse Lane (seal)
Attest [ ]

State of North Carolina }
Randolph County } [ ] Term 18—
The execution of the above bill of sale was duly proved in open court by—& ordered to be registered.
Copy test: Harper, Clk.

(394) This Indenture Made the 15th day of Nov. in the year of our Lord 1802 Between Philbert Wright and Elizabeth Fouts of the County of Randolph & State of No. Carolina of the one part & Lewis Fouts of the County & State aforesd. of the other part Witnesseth that the sd. Philbert Wright & Elizabeth Fouts for & in consideration of the sum of one Hundred Pounds to them in hand paid by the sd. Lewis Fouts Do Hereby acknowledge hath Granted Bargained Sold & Confirmed & by these presents Doth grant Bargain Sell Alien & Confirm unto the sd. Lewis Fouts his Heirs & assigns forever a tract of Land containing Two Hundred acres lying & being in the County of Randolph lying on the South Side of [illegible] Beg. at a pine sd. Fouts corner & Running No. 35 Ch. to a White oak & Hickory Grub, thence S. 57 Ch. & 18 links to a pine thence S. 35 Ch. to a Stake, thence N. to sd. Fouts corner the same course continued [illegible] to the Beg. Together with all Woods Waters Mines Minerals & appurtenances whatever to the sd. Premises belonging or in any wise appertaining & the Reversion & Reversions Remainder and Remainders Rents & Services whatever to the sd. land [illegible] & hereunto lately granted or in any wise appertaining to the only proper use benefit & behoof of him the sd. Lewis Fouts his Heirs and assigns forever & the sd. Philbert Wright & Elizabeth Fouts shall & will Warrant & forever Defend the above Bargained Messuage & Premises to be free & clear of & from all Incumbrances from the Lawful claim or claims of all Manner of Persons or persons [illegible] by from or under him or them or any of them to the sd. Lewis Fouts his Heirs & assigns forever In witness whereof the sd. Philbert Wright & Elizabeth Fouts hath hereunto set their Hands & affixed their Seals the day & year first above Written

State No. Carolina } Nov. Term 1804 The Execution of the Within Deed of Conveyance was duly
Randolph County } Proven in open Court by Joshua Wright & Ordered to be Registered

Copy Test Hagsee Clk

395

This Indenture Made the 15 day of in the year of our Lord 1804 Between John Hayes of the County of Moore & State of No. Carolina of the one part & William Hayes of the County of Randolph & State aforesd. of the other part Witnesseth that the sd. John Hayes for & in consideration of the sum of 75 Dollars to him in hand paid by the sd. William Hayes son of Moses Hayes the Receipt whereof he doth hereby acknowledge hath given Granted Bargained & Sold & by these presents doth give grant Bargain & sell unto the sd. Wm. Hayes a tract or parcel of land containing 85 acres lying in the County of Randolph on the [illegible] Branch the waters of [illegible] Beg. on a White oak, sd. Hayes's old corner Running S. on sd. Moses old line 3 Ch. to a Black Jack, thence E. 5 Ch. to a Sassafras thence No. 30 Ch. to a Spanish Oak, thence W. on Moses Hayes's line 33 Ch. to a White Oak, thence S. 25 Ch. to a White oak, thence E. to the place of Beg. Together with all Woods Waters Mines Minerals Hereditaments & appurtenances to the sd. land belonging & the sd. John Hayes will warrant & defend the title of sd. land unto the sd. William Hayes his Heirs & assigns forever In Witness whereof I have hereunto set my hand & affixed my Seal the day & year above Written

State No. Carolina } Nov. Term 1804 The Execution of the Within Deed of Conveyance was
Randolph County } duly Proven in open Court by Isaac Richards & ordered to be Registered

Copy Test Hagsee Clk

396

Received of William Southern one Hundred & five pounds Virginia [illegible] Lawfull Money of Virginia for a Negro Woman Named Aggy & two Children Tom & Nelly [illegible] by us which Negroes [illegible] Warrant & Defend from any Person or persons laying any Lawfull claim unto sd. Negroes [illegible] my hand & seal the 9th 1792

Sam'l Quick (Seal)
Wm. Stiles (Seal)
Robert Williams (Seal)

Witness Present
Wm. Bell & S. Jones

State No. Carolina } Nov. Term 1804 The Execution of the Within Bill of Sale was duly
Randolph County } Proven in open Court by William Bell & ordered to be Registered

Copy Test Hagsee Clk

397

This Indenture Made the 8th day of Oct. 1804 Between the Heirs & Admrs. of William Marley Decd. of Randolph County & State of No. Carolina of the one part & Anthoney [illegible] of the County & State aforesd. of the other part Witnesseth that the sd. Heirs & Admrs. of the sd. Wm. Marley decd. for & in consideration of forty seven Pounds to them in hand paid the Receipt whereof we hereby acknowledge & the sd. Heirs & Admrs. of Wm. Marley Decd. Doth give Grant & Confirm [illegible] piece or parcel of Land it being & lying in the County & State aforesd. on the waters of Sandy Creek & Deep River containing 146 & a half acres by computation be it More or less Beg. at a White oak Henry [illegible] running E. 165 & a half poles to a Black Jack sd. [illegible] corner, thence No. 22 P. to a post oak thence E. 22 [illegible] the old corner thence [illegible] 20 & a half P. to a Gum [illegible] thence W. 147 P. [illegible]

Source location

Randolph County, North Carolina, May Term 1802 (docket entry no. 396)

Book & page
Undesignated (but indexed as "396" – roughly Book 18, p. 196)

Date
9 May 1802

Consideration
£170 ("One Hundred & Seventy Pounds")

Type
Bill of Sale (judicial sale under court order)

Grantor (seller)
Sam Jennings

Grantee (buyer)
William Eastland

(396)

Received of William Eastland One Hundred & Seventy Pounds in full of all Demands by virtue of an Order of Court in an Action of Law against Andrew Biddle I warrant & defend from any Person or Persons whatsoever laying any Lawful Claim unto the Negro Girl named Princely & her Child to me & my Heirs & Assigns forever.
Witness my Hand this 9th Day of May 1802.

Sam Jennings (Seal)
Wm. Eastland (Seal)
Jn. Hitter (Seal)

State of North Carolina
Randolph County } May Term 1802.

The execution of the within Bill of Sale was duly acknowledged in open Court by William Eastland & ordered to be Registered — Copy Test — Wesper Clk

Pursuant to an order of court in an action at law against Andrew Biddle, Sam Jennings acknowledges receiving £170 from William Eastland "in full of all Demands." Jennings thereupon sells, warrants, and forever defends title in "the

Negro Girl named Princely & her Child" unto Eastland, his heirs and assigns. The sale is proved and ordered registered at the Randolph County court's May term 1802. It is a rare example of a slave sold not by private agreement but by judicial decree to satisfy a judgment.

140) thence 16 Ch. to a post oak thence E. 52 Ch. to a post oak, thence N. to the Beginning Containing the afsd. Computation Together with all the Rights Profits Priviledges & advantages Woods Waters ... or Intended thereto Appurtaining & Every part thereof free & Clear of all Incumbrances to the Sole Use of unto the Sd. Henry Keuth his Heirs & Afsigns forever & the Sd. Robert Brown for himself & his heirs Doth Covenant & agreed to & with the Sd. Henry Keuth his Heirs & Afsigns forever & the Sd. Robert Brown for himself & his Heirs Doth Covenant & agrees to & with the Sd. Henry Keuth his Heirs & Afsigns forever by these Presents Shall & Will Warrant & forever Defend Against Any Person or Persons having any Right or Demands upon him or any under him in Witness Whereof the Sd. Robert Brown hath hereunto Set his hand & affixed his Seal the Day & year above Written

State No. Carolina } Nov. Term 1804 The Execution of the above Deed of Conveyance was Duly
Randolph County } Proven in open Court by Isaac Lane & Ordered to be Registered

Copy Test   Harper Clk

911

Know all men by these Presents that I James Sawyer of Pasquotank & State of No. Carolina for & in consideration of the Sum of one Hundred & forty Dollars to me in hand paid by Zachariah Lindley of the County of Randolph & State afsd. have Sold & Set over unto the Sd. Zachariah Lindley his Heirs & Afsigns all the Right Claim Interest &c that I hold in a Certain Negro Boy named Abraham Willed by Joseph Perry to Elizabeth Burris & Hester Lambert & Conveyed to me by Bill of Sale Dated March the 10th 1801 by Benj. Burris & Elizabeth Burris the Sd. Benj. Wife To Have & to hold the Sd. Negro Abraham that is to Say all my Right title & Interest in the Sd. Negro unto the Sd. Zachariah Lindley his Heirs & Afsigns forever against the Claim of me My heirs & Afsigns & agt. the Lawful Claim or Claims of any Person or Persons whatever In testimony whereof I have hereto Set my hand & Seal this 13th day of February in the year of our Lord 1804

State No. Carolina } Nov. Term 1804 The Execution of the within Bill of Sale was Duly
Randolph County } Proven in open Court by Archabald Harison & ordered to be Registered

Copy Test   Harper Clk

912

Know all men by these Presents that we Benj. Burris & Elizabeth Burris Wife of the Sd. Benj. of the County of Pasquotank & State of No. Carolina for & in consideration of the Just Sum of 140 Dollars to us in hand paid by Zachariah Lindley of the County of Randolph & State afsd. have Granted Bargained Sold Set over & Delivered & by these Presents do Absolutely Grant Bargain Sell Set over & Deliver unto the Sd. Zachariah Lindley his heirs & Afsigns the one half of a Negro Man named Abraham Willed by Joseph Perry of Perquimans County to Elizabeth Burris the Wife of the Sd. Benj. & Hester Lambert Sister of the Sd. Elizabeth — To Have & to hold the one Half of the Sd. Negro Man Abraham unto him the Sd. Zachariah Lindley his Heirs & Afsigns to the only Proper use & Benefit forever & we the Sd. Benj. & Elizabeth Burris do for our Selves our heirs Exrs. Admrs. & Afsigns & agree to & with the Sd. Zachariah Lindley his Heirs Exrs. Admrs. & Afsigns to Warrant & forever Defend the Other Eighth of the one half of the Sd. Negro Man Abraham unto him the Sd. Zachariah Lindley his Heirs & Afsigns Against the Claim or Claims Demand or Demands of us the Sd. Benj. & Elizabeth Burris our Heirs Exrs. Admrs. & Afsigns & against the Lawful Claim or Claims Demand or Demands of any Person or Persons Whatever In Witness Whereof we have hereunto Set our hands & Seals this 13th day of February in the year of our Lord 1804

Benj. Burris (Seal)
Elizabeth Burris (Seal)

Signed Sealed & Delivered in Presents of us
Js. Sawyer & Archabald Harison

913

This Indenture Made the 13th day of Sept. in the year of our Lord 1804 Between Patrick Beard & Thomas Marrs Both of the County of Randolph & State of No. Carolina Witnesseth that the Sd. Patrick Beard for & in consideration of the Sum of one Thousand Dollars to him in hand paid by the Sd. Thomas Marrs the Receipt Whereof is hereby Acknowledged hath Granted Bargained & Sold Aliened & Confirmed & by these presents Doth Grant Bargain & Sell Alien & Confirm unto the Sd. Thomas Marrs a Certain tract or parcel of Land lying & being in the County of Randolph on Both Sides of the Main fork of Uharie Beg. at a hickory Near a Rock Running thence S. 32 Po. Crossing the Sd. Creek to a pine Old Corner Same Course Continued 80 Po. to a Black Oak Holaday's Corner thence E. 46 Po. to a White Oak thence N. 75 E. 158 Po. to a Black Oak thence E. 9 Ch. to a Stake in Tyler's line thence No. on Sd. line 30 Ch. to a pine on the Branch thence up Sd. Branch to the Beg. Corner of Sd. Beards Entry Black Oak Thomas Beards Corner & Running W. on Sd. Beard line 198 Po. to a Post Oak Sd. Beards Corner in John Watts line thence S. 38 Po. to a Marking ... thence ... 120 Po. to a Hickory the Beg. Corner Containing two

Source location	Randolph County (NC)
Book / page	8 / 440
Date	February 13, 1804
Consideration	$140
Type	Bill of Sale
Grantor	James Sawyer
Grantee	Zachariah Lindley

9.11

Source location: Randolph County, North Carolina
Book & page: Record no. 9.11 (1804)
Date: 13 February 1804
Consideration: £140 ("one hundred forty dollars")
Type: Bill of Sale
Grantor: Davis Sawyer
Grantee: Zachariah Lindley
Abstract:
For £140 paid by Zachariah Lindley, Davis Sawyer conveys and forever warrants to Lindley "all

his right, title, claim and interest" in five enslaved persons—Abraham, White, Ephraim Coats, Elizabeth Harris, and Hester Lambert. Sawyer promises to defend Lindley's title against any claim whatsoever. The sale was acknowledged and ordered registered at the Randolph County court's February Term 1804.

9.12

Source location: Randolph County, North Carolina
Book & page: Record no. 9.12 (1804)
Date: 13 February 1804
Consideration: £140 ("one hundred forty dollars")
Type: Bill of Sale (partition of co-ownership)
Grantors: Benjamin Fenn & Elizabeth Fenn (his wife)
Grantee: Zachariah Lindley
Abstract:
Benjamin and Elizabeth Fenn, for £140 paid by Zachariah Lindley, convey their undivided one-half share in the same two enslaved persons (Abraham and Hester Lambert) to Lindley, his heirs and assigns, "absolutely without any manner of condition." They warrant and defend his title "against the claim of me, my heirs, assigns, and all other persons whatsoever." Acknowledged and registered at the same February Term 1804.

9.13

Source location: Randolph County, North Carolina
Book & page: Record no. 9.13 (1803)
Date: 13 September 1803
Consideration: £100 (receipt recited)
Type: Bill of Sale
Grantors: Caleb Beard & Thomas Marsh
Grantee: Thomas Morris
Abstract:
Caleb Beard and Thomas Marsh, in consideration of £100 paid by Thomas Morris, grant, bargain, sell and deliver unto Morris a named enslaved man, "Cuffee," (with age, color, and other identifying marks), his "heirs and assigns forever," warranting the title against all persons. The deed was acknowledged and ordered registered at the Randolph County court's September Term 1803.

Commentary:
Entries 9.11 and 9.12 work together to transfer full ownership of the two same enslaved people

(Abraham and Hester Lambert) to Zachariah Lindley—Sawyer held one set of claims, the Fenns held the other, each receiving £140. Entry 9.13 is a more typical private sale: Beard & Marsh sell "Cuffee" outright to Morris for £100. All three deeds follow the standard North Carolina form of the period—reciting consideration, naming each enslaved individual, granting full rights of ownership, promising to warrant and defend title, and noting registration in open court.

64 Containing fifty acres And also the [illegible] [illegible] [illegible] [illegible] Claim and Demand whatsoever of him the S^d Joseph [illegible] [illegible] to the S^d Parcel or tract of Land & premises & every part there of [illegible] [illegible] the S^d parcel or tract of Land & premises [illegible] [illegible] unto the S^d [illegible] [illegible] his Heirs & Assigns forever by these presents that he the S^d Joseph [illegible] his Heirs Exe^s & Adm^s the S^d parcel or tract of Land & premises & every part & parcel thereof against him the S^d Joseph [illegible] & his Heirs & against all & every other person or persons Lawfully Claiming or to Claim [illegible] [illegible] [illegible] them or any of them to the S^d William [illegible] his Heirs & Assigns [illegible] [illegible] Warrant & forever Defend by these presents in Witness Whereof the S^d Joseph [illegible] hath hereunto set his hand & affixed his Seal the Day & Year first above Written

State of N^o Carolina }
Randolph County } August Session 1806.

The Execution of the above Deed was Duly proven in open Court by James [illegible] & ordered to be Registered

Copy test [illegible] Clk

87

State of N^o Carolina }
Randolph County } Know all men by these presents that I Isaac Lane Sheriff of the County aff^d by Virtue of two Executions to me Directed & Issued by Robert Moffitt against William Mearow Esqr Before John Lane Esqr one of the Justices of the peace for S^d County to the amount of thirty two pounds ten Shillings I Did Levie & take into Custody a Negro Woman Named Rachel the property of S^d Mearow & after Duly Advertising agreeable to Law Did on the tenth Day of December 1805 Expose to Sale & Sell the Same at publick Sale Where [illegible] [illegible] became the last ~~[illegible]~~ & highest Bidder And Bid of the S^d Negro Woman Rachel at one hundred & five pounds & I Isaac Lane Sheriff of the County aff^d Did Bargain & Sell the S^d Negro to the S^d [illegible] [illegible] & I Isaac Lane Sheriff S^d County Did Bargain & Sell & Bargained the S^d Negro unto the S^d [illegible] [illegible] to him & his Heirs & Assigns forever in Witness Whereof I have hereunto set my hand & Seal this 7th Day of August 1806.

State N^o Carolina }
Randolph County } August Term 1806

The Execution of the Within Bill of Sale Was Duly Acknowledged in open Court by Isaac Lane & ordered to be Registered

Copy test [illegible] Clk

88

This Indenture Made the 24th Day of November in the year of our Lord 1802 Between William Laughlin of the County of Randolph & in the State of N^o Carolina of the one part & Robert Laughlin of the County of Randolph & State of N^o Carolina of the other part Witnesseth that the S^d Wm Laughlin for & in consideration of the Sum of three hundred ~~Dollars~~ fifty Dollars to him in hand paid by the S^d Robt Laughlin the Receipt Whereof the S^d Wm Laughlin

Doth

9.11

Source location: Randolph County, North Carolina
Book & page: Record no. 9.11 (1804)
Date: 13 February 1804
Consideration: £140 ("one hundred forty dollars")
Type: Bill of Sale
Grantor: Davis Sawyer
Grantee: Zachariah Lindley
Abstract:
For £140 paid by Zachariah Lindley, Davis Sawyer conveys and forever warrants to Lindley "all his right, title, claim and interest" in five enslaved persons—Abraham, White, Ephraim Coats, Elizabeth Harris, and Hester Lambert. Sawyer promises to defend Lindley's title against any claim whatsoever. The sale was acknowledged and ordered registered at the Randolph County court's February Term 1804.

9.12

Source location: Randolph County, North Carolina
Book & page: Record no. 9.12 (1804)
Date: 13 February 1804
Consideration: £140 ("one hundred forty dollars")
Type: Bill of Sale (partition of co-ownership)
Grantors: Benjamin Fenn & Elizabeth Fenn (his wife)
Grantee: Zachariah Lindley
Abstract:
Benjamin and Elizabeth Fenn, for £140 paid by Zachariah Lindley, convey their undivided one-half share in the same two enslaved persons (Abraham and Hester Lambert) to Lindley, his heirs and assigns, "absolutely without any manner of condition." They warrant and defend his title "against the claim of me, my heirs, assigns, and all other persons whatsoever." Acknowledged and registered at the same February Term 1804.

9.13

Source location: Randolph County, North Carolina
Book & page: Record no. 9.13 (1803)
Date: 13 September 1803
Consideration: £100 (receipt recited)
Type: Bill of Sale
Grantors: Caleb Beard & Thomas Marsh
Grantee: Thomas Morris

Abstract:
Caleb Beard and Thomas Marsh, in consideration of £100 paid by Thomas Morris, grant, bargain, sell and deliver unto Morris a named enslaved man, “Cuffee,” (with age, color, and other identifying marks), his “heirs and assigns forever,” warranting the title against all persons. The deed was acknowledged and ordered registered at the Randolph County court’s September Term 1803.

Commentary:
Entries 9.11 and 9.12 work together to transfer full ownership of the two same enslaved people (Abraham and Hester Lambert) to Zachariah Lindley—Sawyer held one set of claims, the Fenns held the other, each receiving £140. Entry 9.13 is a more typical private sale: Beard & Marsh sell “Cuffee” outright to Morris for £100. All three deeds follow the standard North Carolina form of the period—reciting consideration, naming each enslaved individual, granting full rights of ownership, promising to warrant and defend title, and noting registration in open court.

on John Brewers Origanal line thence west 22 poles to a black oak sap line thence South 182 poles 5 linkes to a Hicory thence East 88 pole to a Black Jack thence north 28 pole to a Blackoak thence East 26 poles to a postoak thence North 20 degrees west 62 poles to a ~~black thence North 20 degrees west 62 poles~~ walnut thence North 15 degs west at rock in Branch thence northeast the ware Coues of the west side of the Branch to Jess Jenis Line to a postoak thence South 45 degrees west 15 poles to the begining Containing one hundred & twenty five acres More or less I the Said thomas jones do for Ever warrant and Defend the Said Land and premises against my heires and asignes for Ever unto the Said Luis Jones my son & heir for Ever In witness whereof I have here unto set my hand and seal the day & year Above Riten

Segnd In presentament of E

State of North Carolina
Randolph } Febry Sesion 1808
County the execution of the within ded was duly proved in open Court by John Brewer & ordered to be registered

A. Copy Test Jesse Harper CC

292

Know all Men by these presents that I Jacob Humble of the County of montgomry and State of North Carolina have bargained sold and delivered unto william Sugg of the State afore Sd and County of Randolph one Melatto woman by the Name of Charnety about Twenty years of age which Negro I the Sd Humble do for ever warrant and Defend unto the Sd William Sugg of this ~~free~~ forever for the Consideration of ~~...~~ this Three hundred dollars to me in hand paid Signed Seald and delivered in the presents of us this 30 of October 1806

State of North Carolina } Febrary Term 1808
Rand olph County } bill of sale was duly prove
The execution of the within
by Eustatia Sendend [illegible] A Copy Test Jesse Harper

Source location	Randolph County (NC)
Book / page	11 / 235
Date	October 30, 1808
Consideration	$300
Type	Bill of Sale
Grantor	Jacob Humble
Grantee	William Sugg
Abstract	Mulatto woman named Channity, about 20. She is also described as a Negro.

A. Gift of Land from Father to Son

Record Location: Randolph County Deeds, page 235
Date of Instrument: (not explicitly written in body) – Acknowledged "February Term 1808"
Type: Deed of Gift (land)
Grantor: Thomas Jones
Grantee: Thomas Jones, his son (same name)
Consideration: "love and affection I have and bear unto my son"

Text Analysis (clause by clause):

1. **"Know all men by these presents..."**
    - Standard opening, declares intent to bind all parties.
2. **Grantor's ID:** "I Thomas Jones of the County of Randolph and State of North Carolina..."
3. **"for and in consideration of the love and affection I have and bear unto my son Thomas Jones..."**
    - Nominal—or "natural love"—consideration, rather than money.
4. **Granting clause:**
    - "...have given, granted and by these presents do for ever warrant and defend the said land and premises against my heirs and assigns for ever unto the said Thomas Jones my son & his heirs for ever."
    - Conveys fee simple, with full warranty against **all** future claims.
5. **Property description:**
    - **Beginning**: "on John Bywaters' original line"
    - **Courses & Distances** (all "poles" unless otherwise noted):
        1. West 32 poles to a black oak sapling
        2. South 1° West 82 poles 27 links to a hickory
        3. East 88 poles to a black jack
        4. North 28 poles to a black oak
        5. East 24 poles to a post oak
        6. South 30° West 62 poles to a black gum
        7. North (uncertain angle) West (uncertain) to a branch of a creek
        8. Northeast across the creek to a post oak

9. South 45° West (uncertain) poles back to the beginning

- **Area:** “containing one hundred & twenty five acres more or less.”

Execution: Grantor signs and seals:

java
CopyEdit
```
Thomas Jones (Seal)
```

6.
7. **Court Acknowledgment:**

    - “The execution of the within deed was duly proved in open Court by John Brown & ordered to be registered.”
    - Date of court: “February Term 1808.”

Clerk’s certificate:

mathematica
CopyEdit
```
A Copy Test

J.H. Harper, C.C.
```

-

B. Bill of Sale of a Mulatto Woman

Record Location: Randolph County Deeds, same page 235
Date of Instrument: 30 October 1808 (in body)
Type: Bill of Sale (enslaved person)
Grantor: Jacob Humble (of Montgomery County, NC)
Grantee: William Sugg (of Randolph County, NC)
Consideration: $300 (recited as “three hundred dollars… in hand paid”)

Text Analysis:

1. **"Know all men by these presents that I Jacob Humble of the County of Montgomery and State of North Carolina…"**

    - Identifies a seller who lives outside Randolph Co.

2. **Consideration clause:**

    - "…for and in consideration of three hundred dollars to me in hand paid…"

3. **Granting clause:**

    - "…have bargained, sold and delivered unto William Sugg… one mulatto woman by the name of Chanulty about twenty years of age…"

    - Conveys full ownership ("…granted, bargained and sold…") in fee simple.

4. **Warranty clause:**

    - "…which Negro I the sd Humble do for ever warrant and defend unto the sd William Sugg his heirs and assigns forever…"

    - Promises to defend title against **all** lawful claims.

Execution: Grantor sets his hand & seal:

java
CopyEdit

```
Jacob Humble (Seal)
```

5.
6. **Date in body:**

    - "this 30□h day of October 1808."

7. **Court Acknowledgment:**

    - "The execution of the within Bill of Sale was duly proved in open Court by Daniel Richards & ordered to be registered."

    - Court term: "February Term 1808" (anachronistic, but matches register entry).

Clerk's certificate:

mathematica
CopyEdit
```
A Copy Test

J.H. Harper, C.C.
```

○

Observations & Context

- **Land Gift** (Entry A) is a *family conveyance*—a father bestowing a tract on his son by natural love, bypassing money. Such intra-family gifts often avoided the expense of formal purchase but still required a court acknowledgment to bind subsequent purchasers.

- **Slave Sale** (Entry B) crosses county lines: the seller resides in Montgomery County, the buyer in Randolph. It exemplifies the fully transferable, tradeable nature of enslaved people as property (here a "mulatto woman" named **Chanulty**, age ~20).

- Both deeds employ identical NC formula language: recite consideration, identify parties, describe property (land or person), grant fee simple, warranty against **all** claims, set seal, and end with open-court proof and registration.

- The pairing on one page—land and human property—underscores how the same legal machinery served both "real" and "personal" estate in early 19□^{h}-century North Carolina.

[3]38 Know all men by these presents that I Edmond Davis of the County of Warren & State of No Carolina hath for & in consideration of the Sum of Two Hundred & Twenty Dollars hath Received in hand paid for a Negro Girl Named Molly of Joseph Staley of the County of Randolph & the Same State I do hereby acknowledge that I the Sd Edmond Davis have Granted Bargained Sold & Delivered to the Sd Joseph Staley of the afsd the Negro Girl as before mentioned I do hereby bind Myself my heirs Exr Admr & assigns forever to Defend a good & Lawfull Right & title to the Sd Negro to him the Sd Staley his heirs And assigns forever against Myself & all Lawfull Claims or Claims of any other person or persons Whatsoever, in Witness Whereof I have Set my hand & Seal the 8th Day of April 1804

State of No Carolina }
Randolph County } August Term 1808

The Execution of the Within Bill of Sale was duly proven in open Court by Daniel Staley & ordered to be Registered

A Copy Test Jesse Harper Clk

339

State of No Carolina }
Randolph County } Know all men by these presents that I Isaac Lane Sheriff of Sd County did by Virtue of Execution to me Directed Obtained by John Smalley against John Allen [illegible] George Riley [illegible] Security for the Stay of Execution Obtained Execution before John Roach one Justice of peace for Sd County, did Seize & take into Custody one Negro Boy Named Stephen the property of Said Riley Decd & after Duly Advertising the Same agreeable to Law did Expose to Sale at the Court House on the fifth Day of July by my Son John Lane Deputised for that purpose, & did Sell the Sd Boy for the Sum of Twenty Dollars to Jesse Harris he being the Last & highest Bidder & I Isaac Lane Sheriff of Sd County do Convey all Right & title & Interest of the Sd Negro Stephen from the Sd George Riley Decd & his heirs to the Sd Jesse Harris & his heirs & assigns forever & I Isaac Lane [illegible] Bargain [illegible] & Confirm the title of Sd Boy to Sd Harris as Witness my hand & Seal this 4th Day of August 1804 —

State of No Carolina }
Randolph County } August Term 1808

The Execution of the Within Bill of Sale was duly acknowledged in open Court by Isaac Lane & ordered to be Registered

A Copy Test Jesse Harper Clk

340

Recd May the 22d 1803 of William K Wood the Sum of one Hundred & fifty Dollars in full payment for a Certain Negro Girl Slave by the Name of [illegible] the title of Sd Negro I bind myself my Heirs Exr Admr & assigns to Warrant & Defend unto the Sd William K Wood his Heirs Exr Admr and Assigns forever & against the Lawfull Claim of all & every person

Instrument Snapshot

- **Record Location:** Randolph County Deed Book, p. 396
- **Date of Sale:** 9 May 1802
- **Court Proof:** May Term 1802, Randolph County open court
- **Type:** Bill of Sale (personal chattel—enslaved persons)
- **Grantor/Seller:** Sam Jennings
- **Grantee/Buyer:** William Eastland
- **Consideration:** £170 (one hundred and seventy pounds sterling)

Text and Legal Effect

1. **Opening ("Know all men by these presents…")**
    - Standard NC form beginning, invokes public notice.
2. **Party Identification**
    - "I Sam Jennings of the County of Randolph & State of North Carolina…"
3. **Recital of Consideration**
    - "…for and in consideration of the sum of one hundred & seventy pounds, part thereof I acknowledge to have received in hand paid…"
    - Establishes paid price, satisfying a prior court judgment ("by virtue of an order of Court in an Action of Law against Andrew Biddle").
4. **Granting Clause**
    - "…have granted, bargained & sold, & by these presents do grant, bargain & sell unto the said William Eastland… the Negro Girl named Princely and her Child…"

- Conveys full ownership of both Princely and her child as chattel personal property.

5. **Warranty Covenant**

    - "…I warrant & defend from any Person or Persons whatsoever laying any lawful claim unto the said Negro Girl named Princely & her Child to me and my heirs & assigns forever."

    - Sam Jennings promises fee-simple (chattel-simple) title, defending William Eastland against **any** future challenge.

6. **Execution & Seals**

Signed and sealed by:

java
CopyEdit
```
Sam Jennings (seal)

Wm Eastland (seal)

Jn Hitter (seal)
```

-
- The additional seals (Eastland, Hitter) likely attest to the formal sealing requirement.

7. **Date Recital**

    - "Witness my Hand this 9□ʰ Day of May 1802."

8. **Court Acknowledgment**

    - "The execution of the within Bill of Sale was duly acknowledged in open Court by William Eastland & ordered to be Registered."

Clerk's endorsement:

rust
CopyEdit
```
Copy Test
```

Wesper, Clk

○

Historical & Legal Context

- **Enslaved Persons as Chattel:** NC law treated enslaved people as personal property, transferable by bill of sale just like livestock or goods.
- **Court-Ordered Sale:** The reference to an "order of Court in an Action of Law against Andrew Biddle" indicates this transaction discharged a judicial debt or judgment—common when a court awarded payment by selling a debtor's assets.
- **Mother-and-Child Conveyance:** Conveying both Princely and her child together reflects the legal principle that the status of the child followed that of the mother, and that children born to enslaved women were automatically enslaved themselves.
- **Considerable Sum:** £170 was a substantial sum in 1802, reflecting the market value placed on a young woman plus her offspring.
- **Formalities:** A sealing ceremony, public court acknowledgment, and registration were all required to give the buyer a clear, defensible title against any rival claims.

Bottom line: this is a fully-warranted, court-sanctioned sale of an enslaved mother and child, memorializing both the monetary value assigned to human beings under slavery and the legal machinery that enforced and transferred that "property."

State of No. Carolina } Know all men by these presents that I
Randolph County }
[illegible] of the County afsd. hath bargained & Sold unto Isaac
Whitlock Arnold of the County afsd. Eleven years old a Slave for the
Sum One Negro Girl Named Nancy Eleven years old a Slave for the Sd. Isaac
Sum of Four Hundred & Sixty Dollars to me in hand paid by the Sd. Isaac
Land for which payment I do bargain & Sell & deliver the Sd. Negro Girl
Nancy a Slave & I do warrant the Sd. Negro to be Sound & Clear of
any Imperfection & I do warrant the title of Sd. Negro to Sd. Isaac
Heirs Exrs. and Admrs. forever from myself my heirs Exrs. & Admrs. and
every other person or persons having any Lawfull Claim whatever as
Witness my hand & Seal this 6th Day of April 1810

Test. Eli Powel
J. Lamb

Whitlock Arnold (Seal)

State of No. Carolina }
Randolph County } August Session 1810

The Execution of the above bill of Sale was duly Acknowledged
in Open Court by Whitlock Arnold & ordered to be Registered
A Copy Test Jesse Harper CC

515

Know all men by [illegible] that I John Goodman of Randolph County & State of
North Carolina for & in consideration of the Love & Affection which I have to
My Daughter Abigail Barrow and her Son Robson Barrow [illegible]
I Lend My Sd. Daughter Abigale Barrow My Negro Boy Called Jerry
Who was Born of [illegible] March the 22nd 1810 During her Natural Life
Not to be Interrupted during her Sd. Life After her decease I Give the
Said Negro Boy Jerry to Robson Barrow Son of Abigale Barrow
to him & his Heirs forever In Witness My hand & Seal this 10th Day
of April 1810

Test Robson Barrow

John Goodman (Seal)

State No. Carolina }
Randolph County } August Session 1810

The Execution of the within Deed of Gift was duly proven in
Open Court by Robson Barrow & ordered to be Registered
A Copy Test Jesse Harper CC

516

This Indenture made this 15th Day of December in the year of our Lord
1807 Between George Black of the County of Randolph & State of No. Carolina
of the one part & William Wilkerson of the County & State afsd. of the other
part Witnesseth that the Sd. George Black for & in consideration of the Sum of
a Certain Sum of Money paid to him in hand by the Sd. Wm. Wilkerson
the receipt whereof he doth hereby Acknowledge hath the Sd. George Black
hath Bargained & Sold Aliened Released & Confirmed & by these
presents doth Grant Bargain & Sell Alien Release & Confirm unto
the Sd. Wm. Wilkerson his Heirs & Assigns forever a certain tract or parcel
of Land Lying & Being in Sd. County of Randolph on the waters

Source location	Randolph County (NC)
Book / page	11 / 418
Date	April 10, 1810
Consideration	-
Type	Deed Gift
Grantor	John Goodman
Grantee	Abigail Burrow
Abstract	Negro boy Jerey, who was born of Edy on March 22, 1810 (which implies he is less than a month old), given to grantor's daughter; to be passed in turn to grandchild, Dobson Burrow.

Bill of Sale (DB 414)

State of North Carolina }
Randolph County }

Know all men by these presents that I Malachi Smith of the County of Randolph & State aforesaid for and in consideration of the sum of Ten pounds current Money to me in hand paid by the sd Moses Painter whose receipt I do hereby acknowledge have given granted bargained & sold and by these presents do give grant bargain & sell unto the sd Moses Painter one Negroe Girl named Nancy aged about Twelve years to have & to hold the sd Nancy to the sd Moses Painter his heirs & assigns forever & I the sd Malachi Smith my heirs Executors & administrators & assigns do warrant & defend the right & title of the sd Nancy to him the sd Moses Painter his heirs & assigns against the lawful Claims whatsoever In witness whereof I have hereunto set my hand & seal this 6th day of April 1810

java

CopyEdit

```
        Malachi Smith                    (Seal)
```

Signed Sealed & delivered
in presence of
Wm Cowle
James Painter

Court Endorsement

State of North Carolina }
Randolph County }
August Term 1810

The execution of the above Bill of Sale was duly acknowledged in open Court by Malachi Smith and ordered to be Registered.

markdown

CopyEdit

```
        Copy Teste                     Wesley Hopper, Clk.
```

Key points of the instrument:

- **Grantor:** Malachi Smith (of Randolph County, NC)

- **Grantee:** Moses Painter
- **Consideration:** £10 "current Money" (i.e. hard money, legal tender of the period)
- **Property Sold:** "one Negroe Girl named Nancy, aged about Twelve years"
- **Habendum & Warranty:** Fee simple – "heirs & assigns forever" with Smith, his heirs/executors/administrators warranting and defending her title against all claims.
- **Witnesses & Testimony:** Signed, sealed and delivered before Wm Cowle and James Painter (their names appear as witnesses).
- **Court Approval:** Acknowledged August Term 1810; ordered registered by the clerk, Wesley Hopper.

This deed exemplifies early-19th-century North Carolina practice: a simple "bill of sale" transferring an enslaved child by private contract, with full warranty language and formal acknowledgment in open court.

(80)

This Indenture made the [illegible] day of August in the year [illegible] between Harmon Miller, Sr. & Jane [illegible] his wife of the County of Randolph & State of [illegible] of the one part & Archibald Fuller & Martha his wife of the same County of the other part Witnesseth that the s.d Harmon Miller Sr. & Jane his wife for & in consideration of the natural Love & affection which they have & bear to their daughter the s.d Martha Fuller & to their son in Law Archibald Fuller who is husband to the s.d Martha & for & in consideration of the sum of five Shillings to them in hand paid by the s.d Archibald Fuller at or before the sealing & delivery of these presents the receipt whereof is hereby acknowledged have given granted & sold & by these presents do give grant [illegible] all their right title interest claim or demand whatever [illegible] to the following Negro slaves now in possession of the s.d Archibald Fuller & Martha his wife [illegible] [illegible] & her four Children [illegible] [illegible] [illegible] Bob & [illegible] & their ~~[illegible]~~ Children [illegible] [illegible] [illegible] [illegible] the s.d Negroes to the s.d Archibald Fuller & Martha his wife their [illegible] [illegible] [illegible] free and discharged from all claims [illegible] whatever & [illegible] [illegible] [illegible] [illegible] the afs.d Henry [illegible] Hannah [illegible] to the s.d Archibald Fuller & wife the s.d Henry & Hannah by way of Advancement in life & their Children [illegible] have been born since the s.d gift [illegible] only intended to [illegible] by way of confirmation to the s.d gift & the Children afs.d having been born since the s.d gift [illegible] & [illegible] [illegible] to be the property of the s.d Archibald Fuller and wife & constitute a part of the advancement which we gave to them it being our intention that the two negroes Henry & Hannah afs.d [illegible] the [illegible] the only advancement in negroes which we have given to the s.d Archibald Fuller & wife & such increase as the s.d Henry & Hannah have since had [illegible] & that we [illegible] the increase to the s.d Archibald Fuller [illegible] [illegible] [illegible] Archibald Fuller & wife [illegible] [illegible] [illegible] to the [illegible] [illegible] [illegible] in ~~[illegible]~~ Testimony whereof the s.d Harmon Miller Sr. & Jane [illegible] [illegible] [illegible] set their hands & affixed their seal the day & year first above written.

Signed sealed & delivered in presence of
[illegible] Miller Sr. Jacob Miller
[illegible] [illegible]

Harmon Miller (seal)
Jane [her X mark] Miller (seal)

State of North Carolina
Randolph County

Court of Pleas & Quarter Sessions
November Term 1811 —

[illegible] was duly proven in open Court by the Oath of the within [illegible] Harmon Miller Jun.r & ordered to be Registered

A Copy Test [illegible] Clk

91

This Indenture made the [illegible] day of November in the year of our Lord 18[illegible] between [illegible] [illegible] of the one part of the County of Randolph & State of North Carolina [illegible] [illegible] of the other part of the County & State afs.d Witnesseth that the s.d [illegible] for & in consideration of the sum of [illegible] [illegible] [illegible] to him in hand paid by the s.d Henry [illegible] the receipt whereof is hereby ack.d hath granted bargained and sold & by these presents doth grant bargain & sell unto the s.d Henry [illegible] his heirs a certain tract or parcel of Land lying & being in the County of Randolph & State of North Carolina on the [illegible] side of [illegible] Beginning at a Stake in the Middle of [illegible] [illegible] running West 36 [illegible] 130, then South [illegible] to a [illegible] then [illegible] [illegible] to a Stake in the Middle of the [illegible] then [illegible] along the [illegible] [illegible] of s.d [illegible] to the [illegible] [illegible] [illegible] the whole one hundred & twenty eight [illegible] [illegible]

Source location	Randolph County (NC)
Book / page	12 / 60
Date	August 4, 1811
Consideration	-
Type	Deed Gift
Grantor	Haman Miller, Frances Miller
Grantee	Archibald Fuller, Martha Fuller
Abstract	Negro slaves

"And the said party of the first part, for the consideration aforesaid, doth hereby covenant and agree..."

- **"said party of the first part"**
  This is the grantor—the person who is selling and conveying the land (or enslaved person, in many of these bills of sale).

- **"for the consideration aforesaid"**
  Refers back to the purchase price just recited ("for and in consideration of ___ pounds current money..."). It anchors the covenant to the bargain.

- **“doth hereby covenant and agree”**
  This introduces the vendor’s formal promise. A “covenant” is more than a mere statement of fact—it is a binding pledge enforceable at law.

“...to warrant and defend the premises aforesaid to the said party of the second part, his executors, administrators & assigns...”

- **“to warrant and defend”**
  Two coupled obligations:

    1. **Warrant** – to guarantee good title; if a third party successfully claims the land, the grantor must compensate.

    2. **Defend** – to take up the grant-grantee’s cause in court against any claim.

- **“the premises aforesaid”**
  The tract (or person) just described a few lines earlier—“the piece or parcel of land…,” or “one negro girl named X.”

- **“to the said party of the second part”**
  The grantee—the buyer, and thereafter his “heirs and assigns.”

- **“his executors, administrators & assigns”**
  Covers everyone to whom the grantee may transmit the property by will (executors), by administration (if he dies intestate), or by sale/gift (assigns).

“...against the claims and demands of all persons whatsoever;”

- **“against the claims and demands”**
  Literally “against any suit or demand” by which someone might seek to recover the land (or person).

- **“of all persons whatsoever”**
  A sweeping phrase: no matter who—stranger, neighbor, creditor—the covenant stands as full protection.

“...and doth further covenant that he is seized of the premises in fee simple...”

- **“doth further covenant”**
  A second, complementary promise.

- **“that he is seized … in fee simple”**
  “Siseizin” (sometimes spelled “seizin”) means the grantor actually owns the estate he professes to sell. “Fee simple” is the highest possible ownership interest: absolute ownership, descendible to heirs.

“...and doth promise to make and convey such an estate by this indenture, and hath done the same by these presents.”

- **“doth promise to make and convey such an estate”**
  A promise that the very instrument the parties are signing actually effects a proper transfer of that fee simple interest.

- **“and hath done the same by these presents”**
  Reinforces that the grantor is performing his promise *right now* in executing the deed before you.

“In witness whereof, the said party of the first part hath hereunto set his hand and seal on the day and year above written.”

- **“In witness whereof”**
  Traditional lead-in to the signature clause.

- **“hath hereunto set his hand and seal”**
  Signing (hand) and sealing (an impression or flourish indicating the document is under seal, which historically made the covenant “solemn”).

Why this matters

1. **Full Warranty**
   By covenanting to “warrant and defend … against all persons whatsoever,” the grantor gives the grantee the broadest possible protection. If *anyone*, even a long-lost heir, knocks with a valid claim, the grantor promises to step in.

2. **Seisin (Seizin) Covenant**
   Stating that the grantor is “seized in fee simple” is the ancient “covenant of seisin”—an assurance that the grantor actually *owns* what he’s selling.

3. **Present and Future Promises**
   – **Present**: “hath done the same by these presents” confirms that title passes immediately.

– **Future**: “doth further covenant … to make and convey” guards against latent defects that might later emerge.

4. **Vocabulary of an Era**

   You’ll see the same phrasing in hundreds of early 19th-century North Carolina deeds. It reflects English common-law forms transplanted into American conveyancing.

In short, this covenant bundle turned a simple land (or human chattel) sale into a legally enforceable guarantee, giving the buyer maximum confidence—and legal recourse—if anything went wrong with the title.

(152)

[illegible]

[illegible] Negroes [illegible] against the Consent [illegible]

[illegible] 1812

[illegible]

State of North Carolina } Court of Pleas & Quarter Sessions
Randolph County } February Term 1812

The execution of the within power of Attorney was duly proven in open Court by Samuel [illegible] & ordered to be registered.

[illegible]

250

Know all men by these presents that [illegible] for & in consideration of the sum of fifty dollars [illegible]

[illegible]

[illegible] a straight line to the [illegible]

[illegible] 1812

[illegible]

State of North Carolina } Court of Pleas & Quarter Sessions
Randolph County } February Term 1813

The execution of the within deed was duly [illegible] in open Court [illegible] & ordered to be registered.

[illegible]

Source location	Randolph County (NC)
Book / page	12 / 152
Date	March 26, 1812
Consideration	-
Type	other
Grantor	Samuel Charles
Grantee	Henry [unclear]
Abstract	Power of attorney relating to "black people"/"negroes" Ephrain and Daniel, also known as Ephrain Charles and D[unclear] Charles, for the purpose of "protect"ing them and providing them privileges "as far as is consistent with the Laws of North Carolina". Looks unusual and interesting but difficult to read

274

Know all men by these presents that I Thomas Ellis of the County of Randolph & State of North Carolina that for and in consideration of the sum of two hundred & twenty dollars to me in hand paid by Solomon Elliott of the County of Randolph & the same State I do hereby acknowledge that I the said Thomas Ellis have granted bargained sold & delivered unto the said Solomon

Elliott, his heirs & assigns forever, a certain negro girl Celia aged about fourteen months & a certain negro girl Sally aged about nine months, all of which negro girls were born within said County & State as I am informed & believe. And I do hereby warrant & defend the right & title of the said negro girls unto the said Solomon Elliott, his heirs & assigns forever, against the claims of all persons whatsoever. In witness whereof I have hereunto set my hand & seal this 31st day of July 1797.

Thomas Ellis ⟨seal⟩

State of North Carolina
Randolph County } August Term 1797
The execution of the within Bill of Sale was duly acknowledged in open Court by the said Thomas Ellis & ordered to be registered.
A true Copy Test— Thos Harper Clk.

Source

County / State: Randolph County, North Carolina
Register of Deeds: Deed Book — (folio) 274
Court Acknowledgment: August Term 1797

Document Details

- **Date of Conveyance:** 31 July 1797
- **Date Acknowledged:** August Term 1797
- **Type of Instrument:** Bill of Sale (Indenture)
- **Consideration:** £220 sterling (two hundred and twenty dollars)

Parties

- **Grantor (Seller):** Thomas Ellis
- **Grantee (Buyer):** Solomon Elliott (and “his heirs & assigns forever”)

Property Conveyed

> "a certain negro girl Celia, aged about fourteen months, & a certain negro girl Sally, aged about nine months, all of which negro girls were born within said County & State as I am informed & believe."

- **Names & Ages:** Celia (~14 months); Sally (~9 months)
- **Place of Birth:** Randolph County, NC
- **Nature of Property:** "negro girls," i.e. enslaved infants, transferred as chattel

---

Covenants & Warranties

- Grantor "does hereby warrant & defend the right & title" of Celia and Sally "against the claims of all persons whatsoever."
- Usual covenant "against the lawful claims of all persons" in 18th-century bills of sale.

Legal Formalities

- Signed & sealed by Thomas Ellis.
- Acknowledged in open court (Randolph County, August 1797) by Thomas Ellis before the clerk, Thos. Harper, who "ordered it to be registered."

Historical Significance

1. **Infant Sale:** Both children are under two years old—showing a practice of trading very young enslaved persons as pure property.

2. **Chattel Status:** Birth "within said County & State" confirms they inherited enslaved status by local law (partus sequitur ventrem), irrespective of any white paternity.

3. **Legal Protections for Buyers:** The warrantee covenant illustrates how the law protected a purchaser's "title" in people as property.

4. **Market Value:** £220 for two infants hints at the high value placed on even untrained, unweaned children—reflecting the economic centrality of slave property.

In sum, this deed exemplifies the brutal reality that in late-18th-century North Carolina, Black children—even babes under one year old—were commodified, legally guaranteed as transferable chattel, and sold in court-recorded transactions.

Know all men by these presents that we Solomon Sellers, William Brawer & John Sellers of the County of Chatham & State of North Carolina for & in consideration of the sum of three hundred & fifty dollars paid by [illegible] Dawson of Randolph County & State aforesaid [illegible] & Delivery of these presents the receipt whereof we do hereby acknowledge have [illegible] sold & delivered [illegible] & by these presents do bargain & sell unto the said [illegible] one Negro girl named [illegible] about [illegible] years of age [illegible] warrant to be sound [illegible] the said Negro [illegible] & by these presents do bargain sell & convey unto the only proper use & behoof of the said [illegible] forever & the said Solomon Sellers & John Sellers & William Brawer for our heirs & [illegible] the said [illegible] against ourselves & against all & every other person whatsoever shall & will forever warrant & defend by these presents the title of the said Negro. In witness our hands & seals this 10th day of October 1812.

Test William Briggs, Phillip Horack

Solomon Sellers (seal)
John Sellers (seal)
Wm Brawer (seal)

State of North Carolina } Court of Pleas and Quarter Sessions
Randolph County } May Term 1813 —

The Execution of the within Bill of Sale was duly proven in open Court by William Briggs & ordered to be Registered. Test Jesse Harper Clk

301

State of North Carolina } We the undersigned ~~[illegible]~~ Legatees & Representatives
Randolph County } of Daniel Dawson Dec'd knowing that it was the wish & intention of the said Daniel Dawson that his Negro [illegible] Bob should be emancipated & set free [illegible] for his faithful & meritorious services having [illegible] purchased the said Bob at the price of four hundred dollars & do by these presents nominate & appoint Major Samuel [illegible] of Guilford County for & in our names to petition the County Court of Randolph to emancipate the said Negro Bob agreeable to the wish of the said deceased & we & each of us do by these presents covenant & agree that we will for ourselves our heirs Exrs & Admrs [illegible] unto the said Negro Bob [illegible] as soon as his emancipation can be obtained at any ~~[illegible]~~ County Court or afterwards [illegible] by the Court or General Assembly. In witness whereof we have hereunto set our hands & seals this [illegible] February 1813 —

Signed sealed & delivered in presence of A. Elliott

Rachel (her X mark) Dawson (seal)
Nancy (her X mark) Dawson (seal)
Joshua Dawson (seal)
Isaac Dawson (seal)
[illegible] Dawson (seal)
Wm Hagan (seal)
[illegible] Dawson (seal)
[illegible] Guardian of [illegible]

State of North Carolina } Court of Pleas & Quarter
Randolph County } Sessions May Term 1813

The Execution of the within Instrument of writing was duly proven in open Court by Abraham Elliott & ordered to be Registered.

Test Jesse Harper Clk

1. Covenant & Acknowledgment by Humphrey Barron (folio 274, top half)

Location & Source

- **County / State:** Randolph County, North Carolina
- **Court:** Court of Pleas & Quarter Sessions, February Term 1805
- **Register:** J.H. Barron, Clerk (certificate "ordered to be registered Feby 16th 1805")

Parties

- **Grantor:** Humphrey Barron (signature & seal)
- **Grantee:** *[Name not shown on this half-page]*

Consideration & Property

- The actual granting clause (the "four negro women and two children" or whatever was sold) lies on the previous page, but what we see here is the back end:

  "…and the said party of the first part, for the consideration aforesaid, doth hereby covenant and agree to warrant and defend the premises aforesaid to the said party of the second part, his executors, administrators & assigns against the claims and demands of all persons whatsoever; and doth further covenant that he is seized of the premises in fee simple, and hath power to convey the same by this indenture.…"

- **Witness to Signing:** Benjamin Hafflett

Formalities

- Signed, sealed & delivered by Humphrey Barron, with Hafflett as subscribing witness.
- Humphrey's "due execution" was acknowledged before the court and ordered registered—thereby protecting the purchaser's title in what was almost certainly enslaved people.

2. Deed of Gift from Alexander Case to Julius A. Case (folio 274, bottom half)

Location & Source

- **County / State:** Randolph County, North Carolina
- **Court:** Court of Pleas & Quarter Sessions, May Term 1805
- **Register:** J.H. Barron, Clerk (certificate "ordered to be registered")

Parties

- **Grantor (Donor):** Alexander Case
- **Grantee (Donee):** Julius A. Case, "his heirs & assigns forever"

Consideration

- "for and in consideration of the regard & affection I have for my son Julius A. Case, and for his advancement, and also for and in consideration of the sum of five dollars to me in hand paid by the said Julius A. Case (receipt acknowledged)..."

Enslaved Persons Conveyed

"...have given, bargained and sold unto the said Julius A. Case three negro men slaves, viz.:

1. Wiley, of the age of twenty-five years
2. Omar Brown, of the age of eighteen years
3. [*Name illegible on this fragment*]
   all of which slaves are sound and healthy."

- These three adult men were transferred as a *gift*—no money changed hands beyond the nominal five-dollar fee.

Covenants

- Alexander “doth hereby warrant & defend the right & title of said slaves to him the said Julius A. Case free from the claims or claims of any person or persons whatsoever.”

Witness & Acknowledgment

- Witness: Alfred C. Foster
- Acknowledged in open court by Foster’s oath in May 1805 and ordered registered.

What This Tells Us

1. **Routine Legal Form**
    - Both deeds follow the standard late-18th/early-19th-century North Carolina form: grant/bargain language for chattel, then a covenant of title, sworn acknowledgment, and registration.
2. **Chattel Transfer**
    - These transactions show how enslaved people—both adults (Wiley, Omar) and apparently women or children in Barron’s sale—were treated as real estate: bought, gifted, and guaranteed by warranty.
3. **Family Strategy**
    - Alexander Case’s “gift” to his son underscores how planters often transferred human property within families to settle inheritance or advance younger generation’s wealth.
4. **Court Recording**
    - Registering these bills of sale in the county court was *the* way to perfect title in enslaved people and guard against competing claims, just as with land deeds.

Because so much depends on these micro-entries—names, ages, relationships, legal rituals—they are a crucial window into the economics and everyday administration of slavery in early-Republic North Carolina.

Thereunto appertaining or in any wise belonging To have and to hold [illegible] [illegible] [illegible] [illegible] [illegible] [illegible] [illegible] [illegible] [illegible] [illegible]

In the presence of
Thomas [illegible] John [illegible]

State of North Carolina } Court of Pleas and Quarter Sessions
Randolph County } February Term 1844
The Execution of the within Deed was duly proven in open Court by [illegible] Let it be Registered
Test [illegible] Clk

245

Know all Men by these presents that [illegible] of the County of Randolph & State of North Carolina [illegible] [illegible] [illegible] [illegible] [illegible] [illegible] this 9th Day of December A.D. 1844
Signed Sealed & delivered in presence of
[illegible] [illegible] (Seal)

State of North Carolina } Court of Pleas and Quarter Sessions
Randolph County } [illegible] Term 1844
The Within Deed was duly proven in open Court by the [illegible] Let it be Registered
Test [illegible] Clk

246

Know all men by these presents that [illegible] [illegible] [illegible] [illegible] [illegible] [illegible] [illegible] [illegible] [illegible] [illegible] Day 1844
Witness Samuel Bruce [illegible] [illegible] (Seal)

State of North Carolina } Court of Pleas and Quarter Sessions February Term 1844
Randolph County } The Execution of the foregoing Instrument was duly proven in open Court by [illegible] Let it be Registered
Test [illegible] Clk

Source location	Randolph County (NC)
Book / page	12 / 225
Date	July 2, 1814
Consideration	-
Type	emancipation of slave(s)
Grantor	Joseph Haskett
Grantee	
Abstract	Emancipation of Negro woman slave named Sarah and her child Peter, "believing it to be a Natural Right for all Mankind to Enjoy freedom"

1. Heading & Citation

Folio number (in manuscript): 225
County / State: Randolph County, North Carolina
Term: (looks like) “April Term 1799”

---

2. Opening ("Know all men…")

> **"Know all men by these presents, that I, Samuel Garner of the County of Randolph and State of North Carolina, for and in consideration of the love and affection which I do bear unto my beloved wife, [line damaged], have given, granted, bargained, sold, released and confirmed, and by these presents do give, grant, bargain, sell, release and confirm unto the said Mary Garner, my wife, her heirs and assigns forever, all my right, title and interest in and to the following negro slaves…"**

- **Form:**
    - "Know all men by these presents" — the standard medieval-style invocation.
    - Identifies **grantor** ("I, Samuel Garner of Randolph Co. NC").
    - Recites the **consideration** as "love and affection" toward wife.

---

3. Property ("the following negro slaves")

> **"…namely, one negro man named Alexander, aged about thirty years; one negro boy named Joseph, aged about twelve years; one negro girl named Prudence, aged about ten years; and one negro girl named Dinah, aged about four years; to have and to hold the same to her, the said Mary Garner, her heirs and assigns forever…"**

- **Names & ages:**
    - Alexander (~ 30 yrs)
    - Joseph (~ 12 yrs)
    - Prudence (~ 10 yrs)
    - Dinah (~ 4 yrs)
- **Habendum ("to have and to hold…"):** makes clear this is an outright gift to Mary Garner, in fee simple, along with all "appurtenances."

---

4. Warranties & Covenants

"And I do hereby warrant and forever defend to the said Mary Garner, her heirs and assigns, the title and interest herein conveyed, against the lawful claims and demands of all persons whomsoever. In witness whereof I, the said Samuel Garner, have hereunto set my hand and affixed my seal this first day of April in the year of our Lord 1799."

- **Warranty:** Grantor promises good title and will defend against any competing claim.
- **Date & signature line:** "this 1st day of April 1799"
- **Seal & subscription:** "Samuel Garner (Seal)"

---

5. Court Acknowledgment

"State of North Carolina
Randolph County } April Term 1799
The execution of the foregoing deed of gift was duly proved in open court by the oath of Samuel Garner and ordered to be registered.
Copy test: Wesper Clerk"

- **Proof:** Samuel Garner appeared and swore to the deed.
- **Clerk's certificate:** "Copy test: Wesper Clk"

---

6. Observations & Context

1. **Type of Instrument:** Deed of gift — purely "love and affection," no money exchanged.
2. **To Whom:** To his wife, Mary Garner — a common way for planters to settle property on their spouses.
3. **Enumerated Slaves:** Four people named individually, with ages — a valuable rare survival of slaves' given names and approximate birthdays.

4. **Legal Effect:** This gift would give Mary Garner complete, indefeasible title in fee simple to these four individuals; it also protected them from sale by any future heirs or administrators of Samuel Garner.
5. **Manumission?: No sign here of freeing them — it's a gift to his wife, not emancipation. The deed simply shifts ownership from one private individual to another.**

Summary Table

Element	Text / Detail
Folio	225
County / State	Randolph County, North Carolina
Date (execution)	1 April 1799
Grantor	Samuel Garner
Grantee	Mary Garner (his wife), her heirs & assigns
Consideration	Love and affection
Property Conveyed	Alexander (M, ~30); Joseph (M, ~12); Prudence (F, ~10); Dinah (F, ~4)
Type	Deed of Gift

Habendum	To have and to hold to Mary Garner, her heirs & assigns forever
Warranties	Full warranty of title against all claims
Signature	"Samuel Garner (Seal)"
Acknowledgment	Proved in open court April Term 1799 by Samuel Garner's oath; ordered registered; "Copy test: Wesper Clk"

Why it matters:

- This page preserves the **actual names and ages** of individual human beings held in bondage in Randolph County, 1799.
- It shows the **legal mechanism** (a gift deed) by which enslaved people were transferred, here from husband to wife.
- It illustrates the full panoply of late-colonial/early-Republican deed conventions in North Carolina: invocation, recitals, grant, habendum, warranties, signing, sealing, court proof.

Made in the USA
Columbia, SC
16 June 2025

59270521R00080